A CAT CALLED
BIRMINGHAM

Chris Pascoe

Hodder & Stoughton

First published in Great Britain in 2004 by Hodder and Stoughton
A division of Hodder Headline

ISBN 0 340 83604 0

Typeset in Sabon MT by
Palimpsest Book Production Limited,
Polmont, Stirlingshire

Printed and bound by
Clays Ltd, St Ives plc

Hodder Headline's policy is to use papers that are natural, renewable
and recyclable products and made from wood grown in sustainable forests.
The logging and manufacturing processes are expected to conform to the
environmental regulations of the country of origin.

Hodder and Stoughton Ltd
A division of Hodder Headline
338 Euston Road
London NW1 3BH

To Lorraine

Contents

Introduction

'A life spent making mistakes is not only more honourable, but more useful than a life spent doing nothing at all.'

George Bernard Shaw

B rum was born on the outskirts of Slough, so things weren't going well from the start.

He was the runt of his litter but, unlike many cats, born into a home that housed both his mother and father. His father was a huge jet-black, long-haired monster cat, his mother a petite and elegant short-haired tabby.

It's a triumph of crossbreeding genetics, therefore, that Brum has ended up a semi-long-haired grey tabby with a jet-black streak down his back and tail – almost like a skunk in negative. There is something comical about his whole appearance, the stunned, wide-eyed look of someone who's just realised he's about to be hit by a meteor, and in all truth, I expect he probably is.

By many people's reckoning of the nuclear family, having both parents around should have given him advantages in life. Good solid foundations, a loving environment – that sort of thing. It's not every cat that has a framed photo of his parents above his food bowl for example (although this may be less a case of strong family values on my cat's part, and more a case of sad and unusual behaviour on my own).

Whatever advantages he may have attained have obviously yet to manifest themselves. Eleven years down the line they really ought to be getting a move on. Brum is the unluckiest, dangerously clumsiest and least graceful cat that you could possibly hope to meet. Time may just be running out for him.

Brum's father was named Paris after the city, his mother Camber after the seaside resort, and Brum's full name is Birmingham, also after the city. That his father should be named after the world's most romantic and glamorous city and he should be named after the grey industrial capital of the West Midlands sums it up well for him.

Paris and Camber were owned by my sister, and so I have a little information on Brum's early days. If I'd had any inkling back then as to how unusual (disastrous) a cat Brum would turn out to be, I'd have asked her to take notes. By the time Brum had shown himself in his true colours, much of his kittenhood had been forgotten. One thing that my sister does remember, and would have trouble not remembering, was an incident involving a very young Brum and a Hotpoint Automatic.

She doesn't know how he managed to get stuck behind that washing machine, only that he did. Trying to climb his way out, he trapped a claw in its meshed back plate. With four other kittens to worry about, he was barely missed for the little while he was gone. It was, however, a traumatic experience for him I understand, trapped in the dark, unable to move or get his front paws onto the ground.

But overall it was the spin cycle that he won't forget.

NASA astronaut training springs to mind in attempting to understand this experience. It makes you shudder, though not even close to Brum's incredible shudder rate that day of around 1000 r.p.m.

I first saw him when he was four weeks old. His general appearance at that time *was* of a man who'd spent time attached to a washing machine.

I chose him immediately, not because of his scruffy long-haired tabby and black appearance or those big round eyes, not even because he was the friendliest of the bunch and made a beeline for me. To tell the truth, and I'm hoping that there are no major feline evolution advances in the next few years and Brum ends up reading this, I chose him because all of his siblings had already been chosen. I'm not saying I wouldn't have chosen him anyway, but that was why I ended up with Brum.

Some people are born with cats, others aspire to owning cats, and others have Brum thrust upon them.

I believe it to be one of life's pleasures taking a kitten home for the first time. On the night I collected him, I rushed home from work, filled the car with old newspapers and headed for Slough with a feeling of happy excitement, and it will probably be a long time before you hear anyone say *that* again. He purred all the way home and slept on the bed. He seemed happy and contented from the moment he arrived. I just hope he wasn't too optimistic, that's all.

As his early life progressed, I became steadily more aware of his ability to constantly end up in hot water. He never did things by half either. He couldn't just fall off a shelf or something, his fall had to have ridiculous consequences. He somehow had the ability to humiliate himself at every turn and quite often manage to take me down with him, making me look even more of an idiot than himself (I really don't need any help in the field, believe me).

Had it not been for a Border collie named Zac, who was owned by my next-door neighbour, I don't believe he'd have reached the age of one, never mind the age he has. Zac was one of those dogs that wasn't allowed indoors. He had a kennel in a shed, but rarely used it. Instead he spent his entire life on my front doorstep.

This dog, whilst a considerable hazard to footing, turned out to be a godsend. Border collies tend to make great sheepdogs, and Zac seemed to instantly recognise in Brum the qualities of a clumsy, dull-witted grazing beast. He therefore decided Brum needed herding.

And Brum was herded. He was constantly prevented from reaching the semi-busy road in front of our flat, and instead driven back into the woods behind. If Brum had thought it all through, he'd have very quickly realised he could have gone over the fences, and got out onto the road a few doors down. Either he *didn't* think it through (incredibly likely) or he was simply happy to accept directions.

I don't know or care which was true. All I know is that, as far as I'm aware, Brum didn't venture out onto the road throughout the whole of his first year, a fact that kept him alive until he was that little bit (emphasis on 'little bit') smarter.

By the time Brum was two years old he already had to his name an impressive history of comically unlikely mishaps and near fatal disasters. I began logging it all at about this time, wishing I had done so sooner.

I've known a great many cats down the years, but I've never known any like this one. He is, for instance, the only cat I have ever seen knocked unconscious by a self-inflicted blow to the jaw. Twice!

He is the only cat I've seen break a window with his head, or fall twenty feet onto the roof of a moving car. I have seen him set his face alight, hurl himself into a fish pond and suffer regular embarrassments at the hands, or otherwise, of small, near helpless creatures such as mice and birds. He has also blown up the household electrics and damn near collapsed an entire room with little more than the flick of a paw. And all this is just the tip of the iceberg.

When he's not causing the problems, the problems come to him. Whether it be fast-moving paperboys, babies with plastic mallets and malicious intent or heavy falling objects, all will find their way to Brum.

Life has been a little unfair on him really, because he is actually a nice chap. Unlike most of his kind, he doesn't even commit barbarous acts of torture and murder, although I'm sure he knows he's meant to.

Overall, I would say that he's probably the feline manifestation of Norman Wisdom. Well-meaning, likeable, bumbling through the daily routine, getting on with life as best he can and CRASH! all hell breaks loose, the place is totally wrecked and Norman (or Brum) staggers around, not knowing quite what happened.

I now realise, however, that those who didn't choose him as a kitten missed out. He may be a walking accident, but he is a great cat and I'm honoured that he chose to spend his chaotic life with me.

This book is a series of connected stories from Brum's life, and from the lives of family and friends around him.

My ambition now is to keep him around long enough to be

able to write many sequels (your subject having nine lives is a huge bonus to a biographer).

Knowing Brum as I do however, asking him to try and stay alive may well be asking a bit much. As back-up therefore, I'd considered writing about his live-in-partner-girl-cat Sammy, but a sleeping cat offers little in the way of new material, and Sammy is seldom conscious.

So, the onus is on the unique and troubled Brum. Everything is riding on him staying in one piece.

No pressure mate.

Fire!

'Nothing is more dangerous than an idea,
when you have only one idea.'

Emile-Auguste Chartier

Despite the lead-in I've already given my disaster-prone friend Birmingham, it's difficult to understand the levels of absurdity he can cause our lives to sink to at the drop of a hat. Or drop of a cat.

Perhaps one of the most outstanding features of his life so far has been his extraordinary ability to catch fire.

The sad truth is that Brum and fire don't mix. Well, in fact they probably mix far too easily, which is a problem. Being a long-haired tabby as well as an incredibly clumsy git makes the naked flame one of his greatest hazards. Sitting here now, writing this, I am amazed at how many separate incidents I can recall in which Brum has actually gone up in flames.

I would imagine that a great majority of cats glide singe-free through their entire lives without ever having to be extinguished. However, Brum isn't most cats. I've now finished counting and I can remember *five* occasions on which he's caught fire, and I've a feeling I've probably forgotten at least another two.

That's an average of one personal ignition every two years.

If that was a human recording those sort of averages, you'd really start to wonder, wouldn't you . . . ?

'Did you hear about that Chris Pascoe, Mrs Dawson? Went up in flames again on Tuesday he did.'

'Oooh, he didn't, did he Mrs Jackson? That's eighteen times that's happened to him. His wife must worry so.'

'I know, liability he is, carries a smoke alarm on a chain around his neck now, you know?'

'Really? Well I'm not surprised. It's just a relief they decided to build the new fire station next to his house. They've got their own key nowadays, save keep smashing his back door in.'

Brum's finest attempt at self-immolation involved setting his head alight, but I'll save that until last. The first time I saw him on fire was during his kittenhood, not long after he'd moved into my bachelor-years flat. Until that moment, I'd hardly begun to understand what Brum was all about. I'd just kind of assumed he was going through a clumsy adolescent phase and that the rising repair bills would one day stop. But, sitting in my lounge watching the six o'clock news, I received my baptism of fire.

I'd left a pan of water on the gas ring in the kitchen, and was waiting for the 'boiled alarm' – usually a loud hiss accompanied by the stench of leaking gas. Glancing towards Brum as he casually walked into the room from the kitchen, I performed a genuine jaw-dropping, full-blown double-take.

Brum was trailing a stream of smoke behind him like a shot-down Messerschmitt. I really didn't know what I was looking at, at first. As he started to pass by, I realised that his tail was fully on fire and billowing smoke. Diving on him, I hurtled into the kitchen and immersed his backside in cold water.

He went ballistic. My shirt was torn open, arm slashed and neck raked into four bloody, parallel lines. I looked good, I can tell you.

Crazy really. To somebody who seemed totally oblivious to the fact he'd been on fire, you'd have thought a drop of water wouldn't have had any effect whatsoever.

As later experiences would tell me, once Brun has found a comedy prop of this nature he will seldom waste the opportunity to use it again.

Around a year later, dinner was simmering on the oven whilst myself and my new girlfriend were er . . . resting . . . in the bedroom. My passion was interrupted somewhat by the unexpected sight of a column of smoke rising from the floor on the opposite side of the bed.

Certain that I wasn't so amazing a rester to have set the bed on fire, and unaware of any Apache tribes living in the bedside cabinet, I realised that something must be very wrong. Mumbling an embarrassing apology and leaping out of bed, I found myself galloping naked after a smoking tabby and again being torn to pieces as I fought to put his tail out at the bathroom sink.

The girlfriend didn't last that long. I cringe when I imagine the sort of conversations she must have had with her friends.

'Did you sleep with him then Sally?'
'Yeah, I did Mandy.'
'What was he like?'
'Oh, he was all right, but his cat caught fire.'
'Oh, I hate it when they do that!'
'Tell me about it.'

Or, possibly:

'Do you know Mandy, I reckon he's a bit weird.'
'Why do you say that?'
'Well, halfway through, he started shouting that he had to put the cat out and went running off down the hall.'
'Oooohh!'
'And then when he gets back, he's all covered in blood.'
'Oooohh, you wanna dump *him* Sal.'

He completed his hat trick of gas ring/tail accidents this year, at a dinner party we were throwing for a few friends. Nowadays, being older, marriage-trained and tabby-aware, I've learnt to always shut the kitchen door whilst leaving anything cooking. But through being older, married and tabby-aware, I'm often totally distracted and disorientated and so hadn't actually done so.

Brum has never been strong on manners and, try as I might, I find it difficult to keep him off of work surfaces and tables. Bad enough, then, that your tabby jumps onto the dining table during a meal for six, without him billowing black smoke and flames over everyone.

I have never seen so many stunned faces. I myself had become so acclimatised to this sort of thing (especially as in between this and the two incidents I've already related he'd set himself alight twice in different circumstances) that I simply smiled politely and asked my guests to excuse me in a 'James Bond about to coolly dispatch a bad guy' sort of way, before marching him off to the kitchen for our now familiar drenching and blood-letting ceremony.

I was able to return calmly to the table, my wife Lorraine still busily explaining that Brum often did this sort of thing and, although the flames were admittedly dramatic, it was really nothing to worry about. The band-aid on my cheek and trickle of blood running from my sleeve may have slightly spoilt the image of cool 007 nonchalance, but there you go.

Of the two other incidents, one is not worthy of too much detail. He set his long-haired back alight on a candle and had a bowl of water hurled over him. His timing was all out there. It wasn't the first time, nobody was resting, no dinner party was in progress and he was put out within seconds of igniting. More one to impress statistically in the long run than a classic.

The other was his pièce de résistance.

I watched it happen, and just didn't realise it *was* happening.

It was a nice lazy winter's evening. Our gas fire had broken down, giving off evil emissions that the gas board needed to check out. We'd called their emergency number and they were planning to come to us in the spring, which was very helpful.

For heat, we'd borrowed a friend's old twin-bar electric fire. It didn't look too great but it warmed the room so it was good enough for us. Brum loved this thing. He would sit staring at it, his nose almost touching it, enjoying its direct heat.

It didn't seem too dangerous to him. It was damn hot where he was sitting, but there were no flames or anything and it didn't look like it would do him any actual harm, maybe just give him a touch of heat stroke or something.

And so we all sat, myself, Lorraine and Brum's live-in-partner-girl-cat Sammy, all watching TV, and Brum watching the twin bar electric fire.

Brum was lying as cats do, head about seven inches from the ground, front paws tucked in and protruding in front, back in an upward arch. He was beginning to doze, or I think now maybe pass out, in the intense heat and his head kept dropping slightly forward and then shooting backwards as he got too hot.

Finally he nodded off to sleep and his head dropped forward so that the top of his head faced the bars of the fire.

At least, that's how it looked from where we were sitting. I think his fur must have been actually touching the bars.

We really weren't paying that much attention. Lorraine had just said 'Can you smell something burning?' when suddenly, with a noise like a great puff of air, Brum's whole head burst into flames.

It's hard to explain the impact of seeing something like that. You just don't expect a cat's head to *do* that. It was like he'd been thinking too hard and his brain had just given up and exploded.

Luckily the bathroom is next to the lounge and there was a full tub of cooling water in there. Brum had gone mad and I just grabbed him, ran full blast into the bathroom and thrust his head under the water.

He went out with a great hiss of steam. He seemed so stunned that he forgot to attack me for a moment. When he finally did, I was pulling him out of the water, and his struggling merely served to propel him from my arms and straight back into the tub.

He just stood there, up to his neck in water, steam still rising off his head, in a state of wide-eyed shock.

Amazingly, there was no real damage to him. His whiskers and eyelashes shrivelled in the heat, and some of those are still shrivelled today, but the rest of his badly singed fur grew back fine.

The fact that he has managed to catch fire twice since that day proves very much that a fool doesn't learn from his mistakes.

And I'm not talking about my leaving unattended gas rings three times, okay?

A Very Brief History of Cats

'History teaches us that men will behave wisely
once they have exhausted all other alternatives.'

Abba Eban

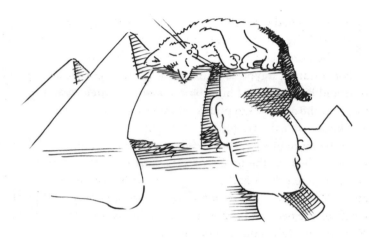

B rum's had a rough ride as a turn-of-the-millennium-tabby, and I've often wondered if he'd have fared any better had he been born into a different period of history.

For instance, Egypt 2000 BC would surely have been a better time and birthplace for him than Slough 1990. It's a well-known fact that the ancient Egyptians revered cats as gods (which, as far as I know, isn't the tradition in Slough).

To be more precise, they believed that gods manifested themselves to them in the image of cats. Therefore they worshipped and pampered them and treated them with absolute devotion. I mean, let's face it, you're not going to risk grabbing God by the scruff of the neck and rubbing his nose in his own urine are you? Not even if He's stained your duvet.

When a cat died in Egypt, it was embalmed, mummified and given its own tomb. They even had embalmed mice put in there with them for afterlife snacks. The Egyptians' faith was so devout that they once surrendered to an enemy to save the local cats, oblivious to the fact that they themselves risked death or worse by letting the enemy through the gates and into their walled city.

The canny enemy, aware of the Egyptians' weakness for our furry friends and eager for the Egyptians to let them in and get on with being slaughtered, had begun throwing cats at them over the high wall. This was all too much for the Egyptians and they soon capitulated.

Had Brum been around in those days, he'd undoubtedly have been one of those hurled over the wall.

In an era of history where you could not go far wrong being a cat in Egypt, you can absolutely bet your house, car and life on Brum sauntering down that road towards those city gates on that particular day wondering what all the noise was about. He would no doubt have had that normal look of surprise on his face as he rocketed into the air, but it beats me why he should have had. Just another life in the life of Brum really.

The above is most unlikely in all truth, as I just cannot see Brum having been in Ancient Egypt at that time in the first place. He has been dogged with bad luck from birth and so I really don't believe he'd have been born then at all.

More likely Europe in the Middle Ages, into a good, loving Christian family.

It was in the Middle Ages that the Christian Church decided that cats were a pagan symbol and condemned them. The persecution of cats became commonplace and cats were actually burnt alive in village squares to celebrate the festival of Saint John. I don't recall that Saint John was especially noted for his dislike of small furry animals, but someone must have thought he'd approve. This all got a bit out of hand and by the early fifteenth century, cats were almost extinct in Europe.

Either out of revenge for their appalling treatment, or simply because they were dead, cats stopped killing rats for us and very soon millions of us were dead also, as bubonic plague spread through Europe like wildfire.

So did people then stop killing cats and side with them against the plague-carrying rats? No. They blamed the cats (and the dogs) for spreading the plague, and stepped up the cull.

It was a long time later that people stopped blaming cats for everything. For centuries they were believed to be witches in cat disguise (if you've ever seen an am-dram production of *Puss-In-Boots* you will know how unlikely it is they could have pulled this off) and it was believed that all sorts of terrible things happened because of their presence. They were not, therefore, all that welcome guests at the fireside of an evening. More likely in it.

This would have been more like Brum's time and place. Although I wonder if he may have been even more likely to have been born before history began.

Around 50 million years ago, there lived a creature known as a miacis. The miacis is generally believed to have been the predecessor of the modern-day cat. It had none of the agility and finesse of a cat of today, and neither was it blessed with much in the way of intelligence.

I strongly believe that Brum may be a miacis.

And, even if he is not a genetic throwback (and this would have to be proven to me), I believe he would have fitted in well amongst these creatures, even excelling in miacis society, for we must assume that fifty million years of evolution would have given him at least a slight edge.

And it wouldn't have been that bad a time for him to have lived. The dinosaurs were a distant memory, so he would have had none of the problems normally associated with Tyrannosaurs and Velociraptors. And unbelievably there were even dafter groups than the miacis around to feed on. I believe that Brum would have chosen this time for himself, away from the stresses of twenty-first-century life.

And when he arrives there by one-way time travel, I'm sure he'll look around for a cosy house to live in with a nice warm fire. He will then discover that there are no houses and that nobody has yet invented fire. Panicking, he'll look round for somebody to complain to and find that humans aren't around yet either and that processed ham and tinned tuna won't be available for another eighteen and a quarter billion days.

Dejectedly, he will settle down to wait.

Down on the Farm

'A wit with dunces and a dunce with wits.'
Alexander Pope

A year of Brum's life was spent on a farm.
This was an interesting period because humiliation wise, it was I rather than he who excelled.

I'm not saying that he shone as a farm cat, because he absolutely didn't. What I *am* saying is that his life merely maintained a kind of embarrassment equilibrium. As he sailed evenly along, maintaining his disastrous course, he was able to watch me fall from somewhere above him where we all of us live, and disappear with a mighty splash into the murky depths below.

This was also a tricky period in our lives. We'd recently dumped the bachelor flat and moved in with a young lady, the new love of my life. It was only a matter of weeks before she realised 'life' meant life, no longer considered us 'keepers' and was actively keeping clear. Our accommodation gone with her, I rented an old farmhouse while considering our next move.

The farmhouse was old, but the farm was a working one. The farmer and his family lived in a modern bungalow at the other end of the yard. It was primarily a dairy farm, with cattle sheds not far from our back door. There was also a chicken coop from which eggs were sold directly to the public, in that old-fashioned and trusting 'leave your money in the dish' way that wouldn't have worked at our previous address – eggs, money and dish would have vanished down the street in no time. Even the chickens and coop would've probably been towed away, resprayed and sold to a bald bloke with tattoos and a goatee.

The farmer himself was a nice chap, and spoke with a Bucks country twang, which is a lazy, drawling dialect. Lazy, in that we simply can't be bothered to finish our words and fail to see the point in putting t's in the middle of them, drawling because there's no need to get words out quickly in the countryside. He had a dry and merciless wit, as I would find out to my cost.

The most noticeable thing about him however was his size. He was a man mountain, a great bearded shuffling colossus. What was even more startling was the size of his twelve-year-old son. He was already as tall as me (a little under six feet) and built like . . . er . . . well, a farmer's son really.

If I found this pair slightly intimidating, Brum must have sincerely believed I'd taken him to live in the land of the giants. He'd spent his entire life to that point in a fairly built-up area. There were no fields or parks in his immediate vicinity and so the largest animal he'd ever seen would have been a dog. When he slipped out of the door and headed for the cattle sheds during that first week, then, he had a shock waiting for him that is almost unimaginable.

To us, it would have been like opening your door and finding a herd of Diplodocus grazing on the lawn. I don't know what he would have expected to find in those sheds, but it certainly couldn't have been anything akin to the group of mooing monsters awaiting him.

I hadn't actually intended him to go outside for another week. Cats are famous for their homing instincts and I wanted him settled in before letting him loose in a new area. And so while Brum was making his terrifying discovery of life on a larger scale, I was stood at the door shaking a box of cat biscuits, as you do.

He came out of that barn like a bat out of hell and bowled into my legs at such speed that he took my legs with him and left my torso where it was. As he streaked into the house I pitched forward onto the muddy ground. Predictably the farmer and his son chose that moment to wander around the corner.

Smothered in mud, I stumbled to my feet, only to completely lose my footing on the slippery surface and slap down onto my backside into a puddle that must have been a foot deep.

The farmer raised a hand in greeting as they strolled towards me. Neither he nor Michael, his son, showed any signs of concern or amusement at my predicament.

'Mornin',' he boomed, 'I glad I see yer, I wuz wantin' a word.'

For reasons I have never been able to fathom – probably the fact that he totally ignored my situation – I too behaved as if sitting in a puddle of cold water in a T-shirt and shorts was something that I did every January morning.

He and Michael were now directly over me, making standing difficult. I would've had to either shuffle backwards on my hands or pull myself up on their coat sleeves. As neither option seemed to offer any more dignity than sitting in the puddle, I was at a total loss what to do or say next.

''Member, if you wan' fresh eggs,' he continued, 'they're in tha' lil shed o'er there every mornin'. Jus' leave six'y pence for six in the lil dish if you wan' 'em.'

I mumbled something about that being great and how you couldn't beat freshly laid eggs, which he thought was a great pun, however unintended. He then proceeded to spend the next couple of minutes telling me how best to poach them.

As the pair of them finally continued on their way, he stopped and looked back thoughtfully. 'I dunno wha' you're doing by the way, but there's a lot of muck in tha' there mud, an' I shouldn't think it's too healthy to be playin' in.'

Before I could answer, they were gone. I was gobsmacked. I couldn't believe that I had allowed myself to participate in a straight-faced, run of the mill conversation while sitting in a brown puddle of God-knows-what.

I truly believed at that point that I had just suffered the worst embarrassment of my life. If this was so, however, it would have to beat off a close contender for top spot only a few months later.

We settled in okay. Brum was happy enough indoors, but wouldn't venture more than a few feet from the back door. He spent many hours sitting on a table at the window, staring worriedly at the sheds across the yard, expecting trouble.

I had a large white van at the time. As it was used for business purposes it had to look clean and presentable at all times. I therefore had to wash it in the yard every weekend. Around a month into our stay, Brum decided that van washing time would be a good time to explore a little further, me being close by to fell like a tree if anything went wrong. I watched him vanish into thick bushes behind the van and pretty much forgot about him.

Len, the farmer, had set me up a hosepipe from the barns for my weekly wash, and just as I directed the hose's high-powered jet at the top of the van, a tabby face suddenly peered over its lip before dramatically disappearing in a huge explosion of water. I heard a scream and then a tremendous crash over in the bushes as the sudden ferocious torrent sent him clean off the van's roof. With an air of resignation born of repetition, I went to look for him expecting the worst. Finding no signs of any drenched tabby landing sites, I gave him up for dead (again). I found him sitting like a drowned rat on the sofa a little later.

That was the final straw as far as he was concerned. Add to that the huge farm moggy, who brought us fresh killed mice and rats daily, leering at him through the window every morning, the startlingly loud heating system and the yard telephone bell that served as an eighty decibel alarm clock two or three times a day – and Brum had just about had enough of farm life. He didn't go out at all from that day on.

Even indoor life took a turn for the worse when I invited a few friends round for an afternoon of back-to-back televised football games and back-to-back pizzas. It turned out one of my guests was terrified of cats. A big bloke, not scared of many things, but with some strange aversion to Brum and his kind.

Brum didn't know this, and this chap didn't know about Brum. So when Brum unexpectedly landed on his lap halfway through the second half of Manchester City's latest epic fight for survival, it was quite a moment of truth for both of them.

Brum must have been propelled at least four feet in the air and his surprised and loudly yelling victim wasn't far behind him. To make matters worse, the ball hit the back of the wrong net at precisely that moment and a room full of stridently incensed men were suddenly jumping up and down and jeering. From relative serenity, the room had become a cauldron of noise and bitter emotion just as Brum had been hurled bodily across the room.

He must have believed at this point that the world had gone totally mad. Mountain sized beasts in his garden and a house full of thunderous noise and angry insanity, seemingly triggered by his simply entering the room. He retreated into a shell, from which my mother made it her responsibility to rescue him.

My being suddenly single, my mother was busy making sure I was okay, bless her, and so Brum was just another victim to be saved on the same trip. Two for the price of one. She felt his salvation lay in 'getting out more', as did mine.

It was due to this conviction that she unwittingly set me up for total humiliation.

She bought us a cat lead.

This thing was a type of harness that went around the cat's neck and under his midriff. Once in place, you then dragged the motionless cat along the ground. It was with a definite sense of foreboding that I checked the coast was clear on that dark night and dragged Brum into the yard. We'd gone only a few feet when he abruptly jumped onto the top of an old eight-feet-high oil container, almost dislocating my shoulder.

I knew the metal on top was rusted and deteriorating badly. My immediate concern was that he may fall through into the drum, this being the sort of thing he would normally do. I also knew that if I let him loose with a lead round his neck he would undoubtedly hang himself.

And so it was that I came to be standing with one arm held high above my head, desperately grasping a lead that disappeared over the top of an oil container when Farmer Len and son arrived in the yard.

I don't know how these two always did it to me, but they'd definitely developed straight-faced mickey-taking into an art form. They could keep me from saying what I wanted to say, i.e. explaining what on earth I was doing this time, with absolute ease.

Len opened with a few comments about the weather: 'Not of'en this warm in April. Reckon tha's them ozones and all tha'.'

I nodded dumbly.

'If our ruddy cat keeps layin' them dead mice in your's porch, jus' throw 'em in the waterbu' and the dogs'll eat 'em. Thas wha' I allus does with 'em.'

'Oh, yeah, okay, no problem,' I mumbled, slightly horrified.

Michael then began postulating theories on Arsenal's forth-coming world domination. All in all they must have talked for quarter of an hour.

Not once did either of them ask why I had one (badly aching) arm in the air. Neither did they enquire why it should be that the lead I was gripping so tightly would every now and then jerk violently skyward.

And, when I thought they were finally about to go, Len looked me squarely in the eyes. His face darkened slightly and lowering his voice to a conspiratorial whisper he said, 'You do know you gotta cat on the end of that bit o' string, do you boy?'

The memory is very painful but I can just about recall mumbling something inane like 'Er . . . yes . . . yes, that's fine . . . thanks.'

As they sauntered off towards the bungalow, they couldn't resist a backward glance. I raised a hand in acknowledgement and they both waved back as they disappeared through the door.

It took some time for me to get Brum down.

It took a little longer for the colour to leave my cheeks.

One Cold Winter

'Through the dear might of Him that
walked upon the waves.'

John Milton

I remember reading a sci-fi book some time ago that featured a cat called Pete. When leaving the house, Pete would try every door and window, checking out the weather from each, before choosing his best option. The book, *The Doorway to Summer*, was named for this activity.

It was a great book that almost had a happy ending. When man and cat had beaten all the bad guys and got the girl just one chapter from the end, you felt great. When the final chapter opened with something like 'but cats grow old and Pete died that year' you were absolutely choked. And then – the coup de grâce – 'Pete never did find his doorway to Summer.'

Oh strewth.

I mention this book for a reason. Not to do with cats getting old and spoiling feel-good factors, but this cat's belief that summer must still be out there somewhere, on the basis of it having been there before. This is loosely connected to the story I am about to tell of Brum and the farm fishpond.

Brum is not a killer, and so fishing has never appealed to him. The fishpond is something to be avoided rather than the exciting lucky dip it is for many cats. He has enough hazards to deal with without walking on slippery rocks around a hole full of water connected to the farmyard electrics (uplighting).

But things are very different in the wintertime. What was once leaky guttering can become a magical overhang of shining icicles, what used to be an old tin incinerator becomes a snowy mountain rising majestically from the shining white ground. And what used to be a dangerous pit full of water becomes solid ground. Tempting solid ground. Misty transparent ground with mysterious moving shapes and lights beneath its surface.

Brum took it all in from his window. The temptation was too great. After near on a year of hermit-housecat existence, Brum went outside to take a look. In the subzero temperatures and vicious Arctic wind, he decided now would be a great time to spend every waking hour outdoors.

For the next couple of weeks his world froze. The pond had iced over and the ice was firm. I wouldn't have chanced it myself but something as light as a cat wouldn't have stood a chance of breaking it. There's a childlike urge in many of us to walk on something so beautiful and dangerous as a frozen pond. It's walking on water, cocking a snook at the liquid beneath, going somewhere you usually can't. But, although Brum was fascinated by the ice, he was never quite tempted enough to walk across.

The pond had been frozen for some time when the huge farm moggy strolled into the yard and demanded Brum withdraw from her territory immediately. Brum wouldn't go. A long standoff ensued, with the adversaries facing one another across the pond.

With the temperature way below zero I can think of better things to do than stare at one another across frozen water for the best part of an hour, but every time I looked outside, there they were. They should have just had a scrap, it would have warmed them up a bit.

Eventually the huge moggy stood and, sounding a high-pitched battle cry, began to advance slowly across no-man's-pond. Brum stood bravely and ran away, his normal battle tactic.

Halting his retreat after around ten feet he stopped and turned to face the foe. Both settled down to stare again.

Why do they do that? Are they receiving orders from somewhere? Why did one start to attack and then stop, the other retreat and then stop? Are they receiving info from the air via robin reconnaissance?

Brum looked a little more startled now. Because his enemy had advanced? Or was it that he'd noticed something very odd?

The moggy was sitting in the middle of the pond.

I feel sure Brum recognised this. There was no real way of knowing. But then something happened that I found equally as strange as Brum must have found a cat sitting on water – Brum got up and started walking towards the moggy. A manoeuvre of this kind (going forwards) had never been a part of his outdoor war strategy before this day. The sight of him on the attack was totally bizarre.

He was distracted. He seemed not to notice the low growling coming from the middle of the pond. As he reached the pond's edge he seemed not to notice the moggy at all. His foe seemed a bit put out by this. She stood, stretched and walked away, coolly and unhurriedly, as if she'd never wanted a fight in the first place and had only come out for a stroll.

Brum sniffed the ice but didn't step out. Instead he made for the cat door, carefully skirting the pond. I noticed that he somehow tripped and fell a couple of feet from the door. Over what I can't imagine – maybe he slipped on the ice or something. One of the genuine pleasures of being around Brum is moments like that. A cat tripping over is a hilarious sight. The look of wide-eyed shock as he stumbles back to all fours is priceless. Brum gets up more like a camel than a cat, struggling awkwardly to find his feet and then lurching up like some great beast of burden with a half-ton load on his back.

I pretended not to be looking. I didn't want to spoil his rare moment of victory.

Around an hour later he went into a state of panic. I think it may have dawned on him at that moment that he had advanced on an aggressive enemy. His ears stayed back and his eyes wide open, staring into space in a haunted manner, for most of the evening.

The next day he toyed with the pond. He walked around its edges. He sniffed it and pawed at the ice. Eventually he walked out onto it, sliding about a bit, falling once, but looking pretty pleased with himself.

Over the next couple of days he got to know the pond well. He played on it like a kitten, jumping onto the ice and skidding about, chasing his own tail and catching imaginary insects in mid-air.

And here the story takes on a familiar tone. It is this type of catastrophe that epitomises Brum. You just know it's coming from somewhere. It would seem obvious this time, with so blatant a hazard involved. But the ice didn't break. He played on it happily for days and the ice didn't break.

In fact, there was no ice involved at all, and that was the problem.

The weather had been warming slightly and on Saturday morning it warmed a lot. By Sunday morning only the thickest lumps of snow and ice remained. The guttering was dripping, the incinerator was an incinerator and the pond was just water.

I didn't see it, but my father – dragged along by Mum for yet another mercy visit – did.

Brum is said to have flown through the air majestically as he threw himself into that pond. It is a sight that I dearly wish I'd seen. What a moment. To be idly inspecting the garden, smoking your pipe and daydreaming, and then to see a cat come hurtling down the garden at speed, bound over the rockery and take a four-foot leap into the centre of a pond. The splash was so huge it totally soaked Dad's trousers, even though he was standing at least three feet from the water's edge.

Brum came into the house first. And this freezing cold sodden shivering water rat landed square on my lap before I saw him coming, adding half a cup of lukewarm tea to his liquid coating. Dad followed, soaking trousers, soaking jumper and a badly bleeding arm (obligatorily slashed by Brum for lending assistance).

We all looked at one another in shock, wet, wide eyed, ears back. Nobody spoke for a good half minute and then we all spoke at once, even Brum, hissing bitterly at Dad for rescuing him. He was still giving him filthy looks from his bundle of towels by the fireside as he set off for hospital.

And so you see the connection?

It's a kind of reverse 'Doorway to Summer'.

Pete, God rest his soul, believed that the summer was always out there, whilst Brum, God damn him, believed much the same about winter.

And of course . . . both were complete pillocks.

Psycho

'Mad, bad and dangerous to know.'
Lady Caroline Lamb

The farm moggy was tough, no doubt about it. She may have retreated that cold day, but she'd merely mistaken Brum's vacuous advance for a fearless charge. Her hard farm upbringing and ruthless hunting instincts put me very much in mind of another cat I once knew. A cat who'd never have retreated. A cat named Peanuts.

Peanuts belonged to a couple I once worked for and spent most of his life in our International Courier Control Centre – which in actual fact was a homely little office in a rural cottage. He's getting on a bit now and had become quite docile by the time I left the company, but in his early years he was a fearsome creature. I can honestly say he was the hardest bastard I have ever known. Far harder than the moggy, and completely out of Brum's league.

He too was brought up on a farm, and lost his sister in a fight with a mink. He used to fight all sorts of fierce animals and survive but was constantly battle scarred, ears hanging in strips, eyes haunted and damaged.

One of his worst habits was dragging home rabbits and eating all but their tufty tail and one front paw which he used to leave, together with a few entrails, on the office floor, probably as a gift or as an offering to God for the profitable running of our company or something. Probably the latter as I can think of no earthbound reason for a company with me at the controls to have made profit.

This habit became almost obsessive. We would forever be finding a tufty tail and one severed paw in the middle of the room. Serial killing. Peanuts was the only cat I have known who could be described, accurately, as a serial killer. I remember at the time we had a very slow, elderly courier driver named Bert working for us. Bert was incredibly slow. He would go off on a job that would take anyone else half an hour and, two hours later still hadn't reached his destination. It was as if he went into an unknowing stasis on every trip, unaware that he'd lost two or three hours and therefore hurt and surprised at your suggestion that he'd taken a little longer than for ever.

Our greatest fear was that Peanuts would one day turn his attentions to Bert. I always half expected to wake to the headlines:

THE DAILY GRIND
Bugs Bunny Killer Strikes Again

New Terror Wave Strikes Sleepy Bucks Villages

The notorious mass murderer known as 'The Bugs Bunny Butcher' has killed again at another Buckinghamshire beauty spot.

The Butcher, notorious for the horrific trade mark cannibalisation and ritual severing of his victim's paw and tail, is feared to have slaughtered and eaten 59-year-old local man Bert Simmonds. It is the first time the killer has struck a non-rabbit victim.

Simmonds is known to have been working in the area as a courier driver. While engaged in urgent courier work, Simmonds would often remain motionless for hours at a time, and police believe that the killer may have mistaken him for a rabbit.

A spokesman for Thames Valley Police said today: 'Mr Simmonds could be very still when working, and could look very much like a startled rabbit, twitching and not actually moving or doing anything much at all. If the Bugs Bunny Butcher had spotted him on the side of the road he could very well have mistaken him for a very large rabbit and therefore killed and eaten him. I believe the killer may have only realised his mistake when he found Mr Simmonds to be without bobtail.

'We also believe that this is the reason why only Mr

Simmonds' left hand was found at the murder scene. We consider this to have been a tragic error and we do not believe other non-rabbits are in any immediate danger. I would, however, strongly urge anybody intending to imitate a rabbit in a lonely location to think again. If it is not urgent and you can put it off until a later date then I would advise that you do so.'

Mr Simmonds was off the critical list yesterday and his condition was described as stable . . . but dead.

Peanuts was, and probably still is, a proper cat. Cool, calculating, vicious and sadistic. I really liked him. Brum did not. He met him only once and just who was the dominant male was decided within two seconds.

I had taken Brum into the office for a couple of hours, as he had a vet's appointment to attend during the day (Brum has a great many vet appointments to attend) and I was taking him straight from work.

Having climbed my shirt and tried to hide behind my head on first sight of the battle-scarred, muscular and dangerous looking Peanuts, he wouldn't be persuaded to return to the ground. Peanuts regarded him with an almost friendly, uncaring eye, showing no real emotion whatsoever.

Eventually I managed to get Brum to the floor, whereupon Peanuts Jekyll become Peanuts Hyde, instantly transforming into a savage snarling beast. Brum took one look at him and legged it, tail between his legs. Peanuts chased him three times around the circular plan office, Brum finally jumping clear of him onto a desk, landing on the stomach of my boss's 'squeeze me I talk' teddy bear which immediately launched into a stirring rendition of 'Are you Lonesome Tonight?' at full blast to an already stressed and startled Brum. Faced with something as terrible as a crooning soft toy, he almost jumped back into Peanuts' waiting claws – luckily thinking better of it at the last moment.

I still retain the image of a slightly horrified, wide-eyed Brum staring into the mechanical moving jaws of a happily singing teddy bear.

But as cool as Peanuts might have appeared to be, he did have a weakness. Just one. Revolving chairs.

That lad just could not understand the concept of a seat that moved. This weakness led him into mishaps Brum would have been proud of. Peanuts would stand and stare at a chair for ages. He would appear to be deep in thought, calculating approach routes, trajectories, velocities, possible landing sites, everything.

Only when entirely satisfied that he had covered every possible angle and that absolutely nothing could go wrong would he make his move. And then, after all of his meticulous planning he would simply forget everything he'd just been working out and hurl himself blindly at the chair, hit it full blast causing immediate seat spin, and be flung straight back to the floor as it whirled around at high speed.

The process would then begin again. You could enliven many a dull office hour watching him at it. We had cartoons of him doing it pinned to the wall. It was his party trick, much as Brum's is staying alive.

Interestingly, when we moved offices, he stopped doing it. He would climb carefully down onto chairs from desk tops. It was a shame. His rabbit habit also dwindled after the move, although he was still doing the odd spot of serial killing last time I saw him, just to keep his hand in.

I think the rabbit thing calmed a little simply because there would have been less rabbits around the place we moved to, but why he should have suddenly sussed the chairs out because of a change of office escapes me. What Peanuts was doing mainly at the time of my saying goodbye, however, was sleeping. Getting on in years, he deserved the break, and so did the rabbits. I doubt whether I or Brum shall ever meet a tougher cat in our lives. I would think Brum fervently hopes he doesn't.

Sammy's Story

'One fool at least in every married couple.'
Henry Fielding

With very little reluctance, Brum and I finally left the farm and moved in with another luckless lady.

I'd first met Lorraine a few years previously, at a medieval theme night, but made no impression whatsoever. I'd been dressed as a knight, and fallen for her instantly, but she can only remember me as having a big round face and swears I'd come as a jester.

Our second meeting came at a party. I'd ventured out from the farm during a power-cut, looking every inch a man who'd dressed in the dark – and on this occasion I made a real impact, hitting her square in the back as I slipped over dancing. When I helped her up, she recognised my 'balloon-like' face. I don't know how hard she'd hit her head, but not very long afterwards she invited me to move in.

For Brum, as well as for me, it seemed like salvation. The farm moggy had never forgiven him for the pond incident and spent most days carefully stalking him, Brum had never forgiven the pond and spent most days staring at it in bewilderment. With so much animosity bubbling under the surface of our peaceful rural existence, it was a huge relief to move back to the edge of town.

Until we got there. You see, Lorraine already had a cat, and nobody had warned us about Sammy.

Sammy is the sort of cat it's difficult to get to know. A semi-long-haired, predominantly white cat with scattered tabby markings, she has calendar cat looks.

Her personality isn't quite so attractive.

She is sullen, scathing and generally asleep, the feline equivalent of a spoilt teenage girl. She even seems genuinely embarrassed by our totally uncool behaviour, as would be any self-respecting teenager.

Sammy is the prom queen, elegant, cool and in control, to Brum's bumbling, spotty nerd desperately trying to impress her and always failing miserably.

If you've ever seen the bit in the movie *Something about Mary* when the outclassed date arrives at Cameron Diaz's home to take her to the prom, you'll know what I mean. Whilst hoping to provide her family with good first impressions, the hapless suitor instigates a chain of unspeakable self-humiliations, including being dragged to the floor and battered by her mentally impaired brother and needing police and paramedic assistance with his fly zip. That pretty much sums up Brum's role in Sammy's life.

Cameron Diaz was fairly forgiving and concerned given the circumstances, so she wouldn't be a good representation of Sammy. (Note: rule out Cameron Diaz playing Sammy if book ever becomes film.) Sammy observes Brum's various catastrophes with a cool and unimpressed detachment. She will occasionally wince and flatten her ears, but only during Brum's most extreme and painful moments.

Despite this disapproval, she seems to quite like him in a reserved kind of way but has no intention of letting him know. She's made it transparently clear that she's tougher than he is and therefore in charge, and that she will not hesitate to use force should he at any time forget his manners. He reluctantly accepts his new housemate. He'd have moved in with the Beast of Bodmin to get off that farm.

She isn't at all keen on me, however. I also understand that Sammy is in charge, and also mind my manners, but have never really got at all close to her (sometimes, judging by the look on her face I wouldn't *want* to get close to her).

Whenever I think we're beginning to become friends, she'll suddenly revert to treating me as a stranger and begin hissing every time I enter a room. The latter makes me feel much like a pantomime bad guy, and I find it a great effort of will not to pace the room, rubbing my chin and scowling evilly at an unseen audience.

Sammy's reluctance to accept me as non-threatening is not her own fault. Like too many of her contemporaries in the human world, she has problems with trust and phobias about forming relationships, due to the thoughtlessness and in some cases downright cruelty of others.

She'd like to trust me but, for now at least, that will not be possible, thanks largely to the actions of one person almost a decade ago.

Sammy was born in Leicestershire (I'm sure I can detect an East Midlands accent in the meow, and come to think of it she also has a fondness for Walkers Crisps). Whilst no doubt being greatly relieved to have been born in the very heartland of a cat-loving country, and over one hundred miles from Slough, she must have wondered what her new owner would be like.

He was scum.

(No, no, not me – the first one.)

Sammy was one of those deeply unlucky cats who ended up being owned by a human being way beneath her on the moral decency and basic intelligence scale. For two years, she was regularly kicked, beaten and locked in confined spaces by a 'man' who fed her and therefore believed he had the right to be as vicious as he pleased with her.

She was eventually rescued, and became the tenant of Lorraine's niece, Shelly, who did her best to rebuild Sammy's shattered confidence.

Shelly had taken on quite a handful. Sammy was now a big, hissing, spitting, frightened bundle of paranoia. She was also deeply claustrophobic as a result of her frequent enforced spells in small dark cupboards. The claustrophobia made her destructive. She would panic at the sight of any closed door and frantically try to get through it, destroying carpets and paintwork as she did so. She was a psychologically damaged nightmare, but at last she'd had a stroke of luck.

Somebody wanted to help her.

Shelly put up with the damage and the frustration of living with a cat that she could barely get within feet of and slowly but surely, Sammy made headway. Unfortunately not quite enough headway by the time Shelly fell pregnant with her first child.

It broke her heart to have to give up on her, but Sammy was still far too unpredictable to be deemed safe around a baby. Shelly knew that if she couldn't find Sammy a caring home, then she would soon be back to square one.

Fortunately, Lorraine decided to take up the challenge, took Sammy off Shelly's hands and patiently carried on the good work.

After about two and a half years, five years on from her early traumas, Sammy trusted Lorraine enough to settle on her lap of an evening. Seven years, maybe half her life, had been wasted in suffering and recovery.

It was about this time that Lorraine and I advanced beyond the 'Dancing Party WWF Smackdown' stages of our relationship, and before long, Brum and I were moving in. Lorraine might not have warned us about Sammy, but she'd no doubt warmed Sammy about me. The last thing Sammy wanted was a bloke in her house.

Despite my best efforts since moving in, Sammy still believes all men to be bastards, and although I resent being classed a bastard by any person, human or feline, who hasn't got to know me well enough to establish that I am indeed a bastard, who can blame her after a start in life like that?

One thing she will have learnt from myself and Brum's arrival, however, is that not all males are frightening, cold and fearsome. It must have been a heck of a relief when she realised what she'd ended up with.

If she'd somehow known that day, that we were coming to stay, her bitter experiences would have warned her to expect Freddy Kruger and Hannibal Lector as the front door creaked open. She'd have held her breath as she stared from the hallway in mortal terror.

And, as the mist from the street swirled in the half-light of the open doorway . . . Laurel and Hardy walked into her life.

That's Not Flying

*'Be courageous! Be as brave
as your fathers before you.
Have faith! Go forward.'*

Thomas A. Edison

M any people simply do not appreciate the level of skill and (lack of) concentration that go into falling. To quote the famous cowboy Woody, 'That's not flying, that's falling with style.'

Which is not exactly relevant here of course, because, unlike the plastic astronaut to whom Woody referred, Brum has never claimed to be flying, but I do like the line and feel that 'falling with style' is very much Brum's forte.

Falling with style, as opposed to simply falling, involves accuracy and timing.

Style is ensuring that your head connects with any hard or jagged lumps of wood or metal on the way down.

Style is making sure that any ground-based item that can be broken as a result of your fall is hit with maximum force and destroyed beyond all recognition.

Style is first checking that you have an audience. Does a cat that falls in the woods when nobody is around make a sound? I would think so, yes . . . definitely, but, where was I going with this, ah yes, but if nobody is around does the fall then get recorded and published ensuring total humiliation for the said cat? *No!* It does not.

And finally, style is making the fall's repercussions look so ridiculously unlikely as to achieve comic status. It is not enough to merely fall over, you need to claw at and take something with you as you go, preferably attached to something else which in turn is attached to something large and unstable, like myself, thus seeing to it that seconds after you land, you are followed to ground by most of the room's contents and occupants.

Which brings us nicely to a fall executed with such style that all of the above criteria were achieved during a drop of only five feet.

Last Christmas, things were a little busier than usual in our household, mainly on account of Lorraine and I having acted with indecent haste once living together. Consequently Maya, a sixteen-month-old baby girl and twenty-one pounds of crazed adrenalin, saw to it that we spent more energy than we ever dreamed we had in her entertainment, and also saw to it that we had absolutely none of the energy we might otherwise have had by keeping us up all night, thus meaning that we had less energy than we'd ever had and were much more energetic than we'd ever been, if you see what I'm saying. Neither do I.

Anyway, against this backdrop of good-humoured chaos and total exhaustion, I finally got around to putting up the Christmas decorations a day before it wouldn't have been worth doing at all.

Having hung the streamers, the cards and the outside lights, I'd put together our artificial tree and started wrapping lights around it. I always wonder about the ritual of Christmas trees. For a start they're a pagan symbol predating Christ and believed to have something to do with celebrating the 'Spirits of the Wood'. The widespread use of artificial trees means that in many cases wood isn't involved. In summary then, they have absolutely nothing whatsoever to do with Christmas or the Christian Church, half of us use plastic ones anyway, and not knowing of any 'Spirits of Plastic' traditions the whole point is somewhat lost. I apologise if I have offended any spirits of plastic who may be reading this.

Anyway, I will now attempt to explain the layout of our lounge so that you may understand exactly how this Brum disaster took place.

The tree stood in the middle of the window. To its right was a heavy oak coffee table and Brum asleep on top of a stepladder which I'd used to put up the streamers. Beneath him, trailing across the coffee table and up over an armchair, ran the much too stretched light lead, plugged in for testing purposes and awaiting a much needed extension cable.

To the left of the tree stood me, arranging the lights around the Christmas tree. It was about 6.30 p.m. and the curtains were drawn.

Enter stage right, baby Maya running at full pelt with a push-along plastic breakdown truck. The concept of slowing down as she neared fixed or stationary objects had either not yet occurred or maybe just didn't appeal and her truck steamrollered into Brum's stepladder with massive force.

Her mother Lorraine, following the runaway baby, screamed as she watched the ladder wobble and teeter on the brink of crashing into the window.

Brum, with his spookily uncatlike poise and balance, simply rolled over the edge and only seemed to react at all when already hurtling down through the air. At this point he managed to grab the curtain with a desperately flailing claw. The wall fixings on the rail were poor, very poor.

Thus it was that as Brum grabbed the curtain, both rail and curtain ripped out from the wall and Brum dropped backwards off of them as they fell with him. He first smashed into the side of the coffee table with his head and then toppled sideways, wrenching the light lead from its socket and blowing the main fuse, but not before swinging around the tight wire like an Olympic gymnast and landing on all four feet.

What style!

As the lights went out and a curtain descended upon myself and the tree, the wire I held jerked forward with Brum's impact on its other end, hauling my already off-balance self face first into the Christmas tree. I crashed to the floor hugging the tree passionately to my chest and turning the air blue with my cries.

As I looked around the devastated room and then at my stock-still stunned daughter, I noted that Brum had fixed her with the same accusatory glare as myself and we were at one in our momentary loathing.

Suddenly, Lorraine started laughing and so too did Maya. Brum stared at me with his 'Oh my God!' ears back, frightened-rabbit look, the piercing shrieks of laughter harsh and misplaced amidst the carnage.

I thought so too. My stumbling attempts to stand and my protestations only heightened our audience's sense of hilarity and I found myself staring at Brum with much the same expression as his own.

Now, whilst this fall lacked nothing in destructivity – what it did lack was height.

Until recently, his highest fall had been from the living-room window of my old flat. This was a bizarre fall and I have absolutely no idea what happened to cause it. I was replacing the glass panel on my front door, about fifteen feet below the said window, and vaguely aware of Brum watching from above. One moment he was up there, the next there was a long shriek, getting closer and closer like an incoming missile and then he was standing beside me.

He began running in small circles, head down, before finally leaping over my car and hurtling up the garden and out of sight at top speed. I have no idea why. My theory is that a wasp stung him at the window and he lost his footing. I base this on his crazy behaviour upon landing, but it might have been the impact of landing that bothered him so. Or just that he's crazy.

We shall never know, but it was his height record at the time, so impressive for that reason if no other.

One fall, however, surpasses all others. It scores a ten for style, it was from his now record height of twenty feet and his landing was one of the most dangerously stunning and funny sights I have ever seen in my life. He deserved an award for this one, not a garage bill (which is all we got).

I know I'm building it up a bit but he really did break the mould with this. To add to its appeal, this was one he did all by himself. The Christmas fall could be put down to a piece of rotten luck on his part, but for this, he had nobody but himself to blame.

I admit I was just feet from him when he did it, and just possibly may have distracted him enough to have caused him to momentarily lose his footing and balance, but he's a *cat* for goodness sake, nothing short of a hard push should have displaced him from that wall and most cats would be too fast and agile to have fallen even when pushed, if you were ever quick enough to push them.

If you push a cat, not that I often do, they somehow seem to ooze around your hand like some kind of shape-shifting entity. It's difficult to get any sort of purchase on them at all. I'm making this sound very much like I *do* go around pushing cats over, so I'll approach it from a different angle. Try stroking a cat (that's better) that doesn't want to be stroked, somehow without their seeming to move you can't get more than a light touch on their back. Their body squirms away from your hand and you can hardly touch them at all. I don't think that Brum knows how to do this, incidentally. Either that or he just doesn't want to. He likes being stroked. He's like some big dopey dog in this respect. Far from edging away from a stranger's stroke, Brum actually headbutts their hand and pushes forcefully into it in his eagerness. His intensity can be quite unnerving for some people, especially when added to his tendency to bare his teeth while he's behaving in this manner.

The overall image is of a manically grinning psychopath. Many withdraw their hand with rather more haste than would be deemed necessary when considering the lack of threat a big fluffy tabby poses to their wellbeing.

Even if you did manage to push a cat with enough force to send it tumbling off a twenty-feet wall (there I go again), what are the chances of it not managing to grab the top of the wall and scramble back up your arm, over your head and away before your arm (now bloody) has been withdrawn from the initial push?

Admittedly, without a push to send Brum over the wall, there was no arm to scramble up, but as I said originally, a cat should never have fallen without the push anyway. Hmmm, I somehow feel I've come full circle here and achieved nothing but start a rumour that I push cats off walls. So back to the fall itself.

We live in a town of hills, and we live halfway up one. Consequently our back garden rises fifteen feet above our back door, and our front door is about twenty feet above the street. The street then drops into woods and plummets sharply to the main road below. We therefore have to climb twenty-two steep steps from the street, which makes us extremely popular with postmen and delivery people. Also the fact that our rear garden wall is now inclining thirty degrees towards our house makes you wonder about landslides. As a local builder inspecting the dodgy wall remarked, 'If you build your house on the side of a ruddy mountain, what do you expect?'

To us, though, the steps and the possibility of our garden wall joining us in the lounge one evening are a minor inconvenience when offset against the excellent view across the fields the elevated position affords us.

At the top of these steps we have a path that runs across the front of our house to the door. The path stops at a low wall beside the door, and it is at this point that we have our steepest drop, twenty feet straight down onto our neighbour's concrete drive.

It goes without saying that this most dangerous point is where Brum chooses to spend his sunshine hours. He will laze along this wall for hours. The fact he can also keep his eye on us through the lounge window from this vantage point adds to its appeal and seems to please him immensely, judging by the stupid great self-satisfied grin on his face as he beams in at us.

But it doesn't please us. We know him too well. The sight of him lounging inches from the edge of a potentially fatal drop are slightly unnerving to say the least, especially as he's twice fallen off the other end of the wall, which mercifully peters down to an eight-feet drop onto nice soft bushes and grass.

One of his lower falls was a double fall and well worth mentioning. As we half watched him from the sofa basking on the wall in warm sunshine, he simply stretched luxuriantly, rolled onto his back with his legs in the air, and disappeared. It was one of those moments when you just sit staring and wonder if you actually saw what you saw. We waited a few moments for him to reappear, staring at the empty wall.

He did so seconds later. Having run back up the steps, looking pretty dishevelled but trying to act cool, he launched himself back up towards the wall. And missed. He went over it like a champion show jumper gracefully clearing a fence. A run, a leap, legs outstretched, and he was gone again, crashing eight feet back down into the bushes.

Moron.

And talking of morons, it also brings to mind an accident of my own at eighteen years of age on a 'lads' weekend' in Great Yarmouth. The purpose of the trip had been to drink ourselves silly, behave like imbeciles and pull women. Since the first two activities pretty much ruled out any chance of achieving the third, we had plenty of drinking time.

And, after drinking for much of the day, the six of us returned to our campsite and decided a midnight swim in the sea would be a great (imbecilic) idea. Racing down to the beach in pitch darkness, we all stopped at a wall.

We couldn't see any steps. Looking over it, we gazed down into a black abyss:

Lad 1: What d'yer reckonishh down there?
Lad 2: The beach yoush darsht shod!
Lad 3: But how far down ish it? Hic, it could be a really high wall.
Me: Thersh only one way to find out! Geronishmo!

I vaulted the wall and felt like I was falling for ever. Down and down I fell, finally coming roughly to rest in a clump of tearing, brambly plants on a sand dune.

Lad 3: Chrishh?
Me: –
Lad 4: Ish he dead?
Lad 2: *Oi! Are you dead?*
Me: No.
Lad 2: *No?*
Me: No, ish absholutely fine. Ish jush a few feet drop. C'mon down here.

CRASH CRASH CRASH CRASH CRASH.

I listened in drunken glee as my mates came crashing down all around.

Until one landed on me, knocking his tooth out and cutting my head open. No matter. We hardly noticed and raced down to the dark sea, anaesthetised, torn, battered, bleeding shark bait.

I often wonder how most men of twenty-five ever get to be that age, I really do.

Anyway, the big fall, Brum's fall, spectacular and death-defying. I mentioned I might have distracted him. There was no might about it. I distracted him.

Stamping on an empty Ribena carton two yards away from him, causing a huge report that echoed across the rooftops, would have been distracting, I admit. I just wasn't thinking beyond that carton. Ribena carton – Foot – Foot – Ribena carton. Hah! BANG!

Brum shot up, hair in the air, lost his footing, stumbled and, shooting me a horrified glance, fell backwards off the highest point of the wall.

As he did so, I heard my neighbour's car start to move down the drive. Oh my God, I thought, this is finally it for him. He's going to hit that concrete at breakneck speed and then be run over by my neighbour's car just to make sure. That would be about right.

My neighbour shot out into the road without stopping, I guessed he must have hit him and not realised. And then I saw it.

My neighbour was driving off down the road with Brum riding his car like some Bondi Beach surfer. My jaw dropped open. The sight was truly unbelievable. You just don't often see a Vauxhall Astra motoring away with a tabby standing on its roof, ears back, eyes fixed straight ahead, the wind sweeping back its long fur.

I thought about shouting but it was too late, he was out of range with his car radio booming. I watched as my neighbour pulled to a sudden halt to let another car by. A flying tabby catapulted from his roof and into the bushes on the opposite side of the road.

My neighbour pulled over. He must have seen him go. He got out very slowly, his arms slightly bowed from his side in a gesture of 'What the . . . ?' He stared into the thicket for a few moments and finally saw an extremely pissed off Brum emerge and run back across the road. My neighbour looked around in bemusement and spotted me, looking down the road at him from the wall. I waved. He tentatively waved back.

We stared at one another for a few moments and finally he shouted up, 'Where did he come from? He flew over my car . . . I think I must have hit him or something . . .'

'No, no!' I called back, 'It's okay, he was on your roof.'

He looked at his roof, we both noticed the dent for the first time. His radio had obviously been loud enough to mask the sound of sixteen pounds of tabby landing on him.

This, I believe, was 'falling with style' in its purest form. No fall could have been more comical and perfectly timed had it been choreographed.

And just for a moment, as the car braked and he was hurled into the bushes, it went beyond that.

For a moment, he actually flew.

Where Sparrows Dare

'Expect problems and eat them for breakfast.'
Alfred A. Montapert

I have spoken often about Brum's total failure to be a proper cat. From a distance you would doubt your eyesight. You'd swear that you were looking at the general outline of a cat, but surely cats move with slinky finesse. They wouldn't just fall over like that, and was that an optical illusion or did it just walk straight into a tree.

A cat wouldn't do these things. But Brum would, and usually does.

With his unfortunate farm days well behind him and an optimistic future stretching ahead, his next trick was to become embroiled in a long drawn-out war . . . with a sparrow. Any real cat would have dispatched that sparrow on the day hostilities began. If cat–sparrow wars were to make the newspapers, the *Times* would probably have reported: 'SPARROW SURRENDERS – after almost five seconds of ferocious paw to wing fighting yesterday the sparrow has unconditionally surrendered. No quarter was given however, and after much cuffing around, a bloodbath is feared to have ensued.'

The tabloids would no doubt have said: 'SPARROW'S MUM IS SEX CRAZED OPIUM FIEND – Mrs Sparrow has eaten poppy seeds and continues to have relationships with OTHER SPARROWS, your on-the-spot *Daily Stuff* can reveal today. Sparrow Junior declined to comment, however, having just been eaten by a cat.'

Not so for Brum. Not only was the war not over in a day, not only did he allow it to drag on for over a month, he eventually, somehow, managed to lose it. From the first tentative exchanges until the last bitter days of fighting a month later, Brum did not, as far as I know, ever win a battle.

True, the sparrow always had total air superiority, but on the ground, where it mattered, you would have expected Brum to at least have held his own. But by the end of the war he'd surrendered all but his indoor territory to the sparrow.

Exactly how the war began is uncertain, but what is known is that Brum has a penchant for climbing trees. Out of compassion you'd hope that a creature with his track record for bumps and bruises would keep well away from so obvious a danger as the high branches of a tree, but sadly not. I believe that during one of his climbing expeditions that year he may well have stumbled upon his would-be adversary's nest. I doubt he'd have done any damage deliberately but in his case damage would have been likely nonetheless, if not inevitable.

I have a mental picture of him tripping over it and then ripping it to pieces while trying frantically to regain his hold on the branch. But that's just conjecture. Whatever the reason (probably the sparrow protecting its eggs or young initially), this sparrow very suddenly took a violent dislike to Brum.

Our kitchen window looks down onto a flat roof, a sunny spot where Brum often sits when Sammy's occupying his favoured front wall. I first became aware that Brum was having bird problems when he scrambled over the lip of this roof and into my view from the window. His face was a mask of abject wide-eyed terror. He stopped and swiped at the air.

It took me a few moments to realise that he was being dive bombed by a sparrow. The sparrow's attacks got more and more daring as it realised that its feline foe's reactions were not those which would normally be expected of a swift-moving predator. More those of a sedated sheep or house brick. In fact, the sparrow was able to get close enough to peck at the back of Brum's head on two occasions before he even turned to face the direction of its attacks.

Getting close to a wall to protect himself was a smart move by Brum. Sitting staring at it while attacks came in from behind was not.

The sparrow's bombardment continued and Brum's air defence systems (consisting chiefly of swipes at the airspace previously occupied by the sparrow) proved ineffective. Brum was eventually forced from the roof and through his cat door. He'd lost treasured territory to his enemy, and he'd lose very much more ground, and face, in the weeks to come.

The sparrow's campaign was relentless during the following month until one memorable afternoon in early June. A battle-weary Brum was caught on top of a fence dividing our garden from next door's. Our neighbour (our 'other' neighbour. A neighbour with an undamaged car but lacking Brum awareness training), a nice chap and keen gardener, had recently constructed a stretchy-type-plastic system of low level coverings supported by short wooden uprights to protect his plants from pests exactly like the two combatants of our story.

He was working in his garden at the time of this latest altercation and oblivious to the rapidly unfolding drama taking place above his head. His first indication that something was amiss – the sudden screeching of the sparrow overhead.

Looking up, he spotted Brum crouched low on top of the fence, and assumed that the cat was bothering the bird. Well, you would wouldn't you?

Seconds later Brum hurtled sideways from the sky. Sideways. Cats always land on all fours, but Brum dropped sideways.

He landed with a heavy thud, slap bang in the middle of the so recently and painstakingly constructed greenhouse system. The sudden combination of impact and weight pulled the wooden supports inwards and immediately trapped Brum in a plastic cocoon. He thrashed madly, wildly, totally destroying both plastic and plants in a frenzied bid for freedom.

My neighbour stood motionless and observed all of this in what he later described as a kind of grim resignation.

At this point the sparrow resumed its attack, much to my neighbour's astonishment, who hadn't known Brum long enough to know that these things were possible. And then came the coup de grâce. The sparrow actually alighted onto Brum's back to casually peck at his ear. The battle was halted by our neighbour who found himself in the unprecedented position of rescuing a cat from a small bird.

Brum didn't go out for a while after that. We wondered briefly if we should buy him a tin helmet for future excursions, but I doubt if he would have worn it.

Months later, we spotted Brum lying out on his suntrap roof. About five feet from him sat the sparrow.

The war was over.

Incompetence

'When can their glory fade?
O' the wild charge they made!'

From 'The Charge of the Light Brigade'
Alfred, Lord Tennyson

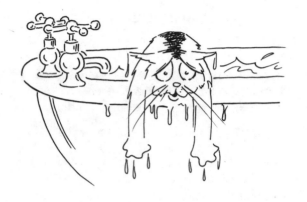

L orraine is Queen of the Comic Put-Down. She will often leave me speechless in an exchange, knowing full well that my next line had better be damn good or it's going to sound pretty silly straight after her masterpiece.

This morning she did it again. I had managed to turn a winning situation for us into absolute defeat, with just a few deft and daft manoeuvres. I could tell that Lorraine was impressed.

As I tried, falteringly, to explain my mistake, she put her hand on my shoulder, shushed me, smiled, and told me, 'Darling, I love you for your sheer blundering incompetence.'

And with that the matter was closed. A stinging rebuke delivered as one would pay a supreme compliment. I pointed a finger but couldn't think of anything to add. She'd done it again.

Sheer blundering incompetence.

Yes. I'd admit that summed it up well. At a stroke I'd wasted money and thrown in the promise of more wasted money at a later date. Absolute sheer blundering incompetence. Not of the kind my tabby friend could ever have aspired to. He has cost us money. He's broken a fair few valuable items and damaged cars, but never just given it away to anyone who asked for it.

He doesn't have the scope for incompetence that we humans have. The more intelligent and capable the life form, the greater levels of stupidity and incapability it may rise to. What immediately springs to mind when I ponder incompetence is an incident that occurred in Scotland during the run in to a General Election. One of the major parties had assembled the press and a small crowd for the unveiling of their new national billboard campaign. The huge billboard in question was draped in ceremonial curtains behind a makeshift podium. Speeches were made and the cord was pulled.

The curtains swung open to reveal not the planned propaganda poster but . . . a gigantic Tesco's ad, complete with special offers and directions to a local store. As the audience gawped in bewildered silence and press cameras flashed away, getting far better pictures than they could ever have hoped for, the politician attempted to make light of it all. But he must have been absolutely livid.

The most awe-inspiring thing about this mistake is how it could have ever happened in the first place. How did highly paid advertising executives manage to centre all of this national attention on a poster so obviously not the one they themselves had designed? Didn't they notice it? Wasn't it big enough?

A team of craftsmen then spend hours constructing a stage around the thirty-foot Tesco's ad and still nobody notices the error. How did they continue not to see it when their faces were virtually pressed against the thing as they hung curtains on it?

I doubt very much that the politician ended up placing his hand on the culprit's shoulder and telling him that he loved him for his sheer blundering incompetence. But then again . . .

Now, had Brum been human I'm sure he could have run to something as elaborate as all of that, but sadly he just won't get the opportunity. Major political parties are unlikely to come to him for help and advice with image enhancement issues.

There are many things in the human world that if available to Brum, would greatly broaden his range for possible disaster. One thing that would certainly do it would be an automobile. If he can damage a car without even being behind the wheel, imagine what he could do driving one. Brum in control of a great heavy fast moving lump of metal is a terrifying thought.

And yet, we let other incompetents drive them. An ex-colleague of mine, who it would be a little unfair to describe as incompetent, would have to hold his hands up and admit he shouldn't have been behind the wheel on his first day at the courier company I managed.

He eventually went on to run a successful transport business, but his debut for us could only have been marginally more embarrassing had he turned up to work without his trousers on.

Having collected his first ever consignment, he set off on a short trip from High Wycombe in Bucks to Staines in Middlesex, a thirty-five minute journey of around twenty miles. Four and a half hours later and having covered 132 traffic clogged miles, he arrived at his destination.

On a route that should have taken him via just two junctions of the M25 motorway, he had managed to see twenty-nine of its thirty junctions, travel first over and then under the River Thames and pass through six counties.

All of this had been achieved through a combination of good advice (that a good route would be down the M4 and onto the M25) and a confident and unshakable, but utterly stupid belief that the M25 was only navigable in a clockwise direction. Hence having arrived at the motorway, with Staines ten miles to the south, he headed north, then east, then south, then west and finally north again, covering almost the entire circuit of the motorway.

The thing that has always bothered me about this was what on earth he thought the cars on the opposite carriageway were doing?

Apart from the cars in front of him, he could have seen nothing else but oncoming traffic to his right all morning. Did it not cross his mind, even once, that they were all going *anti-clockwise*? Did their presence over there not offer him just a tiny clue that his preconception of the motorway may have been absolute nonsense? Maybe he thought it had all been done with mirrors. The disturbing thing is that such a powerful mind was in charge of a three and a half ton vehicle.

Nevertheless, I am grateful to him for the entertainment.

Another advantage to humans in incompetence scope is access to alcohol. Brum's never been interested in the stuff, and that's a very good thing. In his very early days, I saw him befuddled by the after-effects of an anaesthetic and so fully realise the implications of a drunken Brum.

Having been under the knife in the morning, he came back from the vet's mid-afternoon. Within minutes of arriving home, he'd twice missed an armchair, hitting a standard lamp on his first approach and toppling a vase on his second. Having been carefully placed on his desired armchair, he then rolled off and knocked a cup of tea over.

A little later he jumped into a bath of hot water, much to my then lodger's surprise, who was occupying the bath at the time and almost had his chance of fatherhood horrifically removed in the ensuing struggle. It would have been a timely revenge on the human race if that had happened. It was precisely that sort of thing that'd seen Brum anaesthetised in the first place.

You would have to say that jumping into the bath may not have totally been down to his state of chemical confusion. He has often jumped into full baths and it is normally down to a condition he suffers from that we call 'solid universe theory'. You see, Brum believes that nothing changes from one hour to the next, that the universe is a constant. He'd been sitting in the bath in the morning, and it was dry, therefore so would it be in the evening.

The bath is a constant, so must be its contents. His faith in this theory seems resolute, despite huge bodies of evidence (and small bodies of water) to the contrary. He therefore feels no need to glance into a bath to check if it is empty or full. Logic tells him the bath must be empty, so he simply jumps straight over the side and damn near drowns.

The anaesthetic-related shenanigans drew to a close after the bathroom brawl. Weaving out of the door like a drowned and drunken rat, he collapsed to the floor in a wet heap, almost being trampled as my swearing lodger stumbled out behind him, bleeding from leg and stomach scratches and mumbling about sharks.

It makes you realise that Brum would be listed as a dangerous species if he ever got his hands on a bottle or two, but human-wise I have never seen the services of alcohol to comedy more adequately demonstrated than by a friend of mine during the World Cup 1998.

If there could ever be a parallel of Brum in the human world, it is quite definitely you, Andrew Bond.

We'd all gone down to the coast to watch the early afternoon England opener against Tunisia in a huge football orientated pub. There were flags and large screens everywhere, and incredibly tight security. We'd all been damn near strip-searched on the way in and warned in no uncertain terms, by the huge and unsmiling doorman, of the consequences of swearing, aggressive behaviour, breathing and most especially narcotic abuse. He seemed pretty angry about even mentioning the word 'narcotic', as if he'd had enough problems with *that* issue already and he would take not one more bit of it.

I don't know what the matter with Andy was that day, but he was slurring after one drink. As the queues at the bar were massive, it suddenly occurred to Andy that the big four-pint jugs that sports bars often do (so you can get a whole game's worth in at once) would be a better idea than keep struggling to the bar. Leaning over a low balcony beside our seats, he attracted the door-monster's attention by tapping him on the top of his shaven head.

The monster jumped, slightly startled, and did not look at all amused. I thought he was going to clump Andy one there and then, but instead he stared morosely and waited to hear what he had to say.

Andy, very pleasantly, asked him if they did jugs in the pub. Only he didn't say that at all. We all heard his slurry voice mispronounce the crucial word. Consequently he asked the already rattled bouncer, 'Do you do drugs in this pub mate?'

The monster blinked, unsure he could have heard correctly. So did we. Unaware of a problem, Andy continued, 'Only what with the queues, I thought it would be easier if I got some drugs . . . It'd save keep going to the bar.'

I'd never seen anybody lifted by the throat and dragged over a balcony before. The monster took quite a bit of calming down, but eventually he put Andy down and we watched the game.

Unbelievably, a few minutes before half time, Andy, who was

now barely coherent and with a pint sloshing dangerously in his hand, leant over and tapped the doorman on the head again, wanting to know where the gents were.

As the doorman looked up, he was greeted by a face full of lager from somebody appearing to call him a 'toilet'. Protests of innocence no longer withstanding, we very quickly found ourselves outside on the pavement and looking for another pub. By the time we found one that wasn't heaving full, England had won 2–0 and another game had started – Colombia v. Romania. Both teams normally play in yellow, so Romania were in a second kit. The following exchange of words is worth noting simply to demonstrate exactly how drunk Andy was by this time:

Andy: Wash game ish thish?

Barman: Romania and Colombia.

Andy: Ish it?

Barman: Yeah, still o–o at the moment.

Andy: (*squinting hard at TV screen*) I had no idea thersh wash so many black people in Romania.

Barman: Er . . . no, no mate. That's Colombia in the yellow.

Andy: Oh, sorry yesh. Yesh. When are the Romanians playing then?

And so on. He wisely stopped drinking at this point, but the rot had set in, and the sequence of events as we left the pub ensured that the story of his day would be told whenever his friends gathered, from that day forward and forever.

A huge group of girls in England warpaint and shirts were on the opposite side of the road as we exited the pub door. Andy, still half drunk and beer-bold, shouted some inane greeting to them and was cheered for his efforts. Raising a hand in the air and heading towards them, he failed to appreciate that he was at the top of a flight of concrete steps.

He stepped into thin air and tumbled rapidly downwards, stylishly completing a double somersault before landing heavily on his back on the pavement.

His new friends howled with laughter as he clambered back to his feet, making light of it all, laughing and joking, somehow believing that he was still in with a chance. He staggered across the pavement towards the road, limping and clearly in great discomfort.

Stepping off the high curb, he promptly yelled in pain as his ankle buckled beneath him and he fell into the gutter. The girls opposite were helpless with laughter. A small crowd had now gathered to see what all the fuss was about.

Now deeply embarrassed, Andy was still trying to make a joke of it all as he staggered up and walked straight in front of a taxi in the middle of the road. The taxi mercifully dealt him a heavy blow, and we desperately hoped that this would deter him from pressing further forward but, spinning on his feet, he amazingly still attempted to make it to the opposite side of the road.

It was like an heroic charge in a war movie, a fatally wounded Steve McQueen stumbling on towards the enemy bunker, bullet after bullet finding its mark but failing to stop him. I'm quite sure a few bullets wouldn't have stopped Andy either. He'd have sunk to his knees in a pool of blood in front of the first girl he reached, and with his dying breath asked her if she came to this stretch of pavement often and fancied showing him the local nightlife or something.

But it wasn't to be. Andy's charge, as it has come to be known, was humiliatingly halted by an enraged taxi driver screaming abuse at him and many people rushing up to see if he needed an ambulance. With all this going on over his shoulder, he still attempted to chat to the now rapidly retreating girls.

I have often read that doomed charges like those of the Light Brigade and by the Confederate Army at Gettysburg are amongst the most tragically moving and stunningly beautiful sights that it is possible to see.

I now know that to be true.

Brummy Jones's Diary

'The road to hell is paved with good intentions.'

Proverb

The diary of a tabby-something singleton.

New Year's Resolutions

I Will Not

Smoke (i.e. catch fire).
Vomit upon more than two fabric surfaces per day.
Behave clumsily around the house, but instead imagine others are
    watching (and taking notes for book).
Get annoyed with the white cat or the baby.
Regurgitate more than I eat.
Allow smaller and more helpless creatures to take liberties.
Fall heavily, but instead fall with poise and grace.
Die.
Get very wet, but instead remain dry and elegant.
Obsess about the white cat, as pathetic to have crush on cat who
    holds me in contempt and may kill me.

I Will

Not vomit upon more than two fabric surfaces per day.
Stop smoking.
Reduce overall mass by around 3½" by simply distributing excess
    fur around house.
Catch a bird, without it turning the tables on me.

Donate all fur, not properly attached, to the baby for her hidden
   collection.
Be more assertive.
Lie down straight away when I get up in the morning.
Form functional relationships with the white cat and the baby.
Climb trees twice weekly not merely to *look* at sparrows.
Learn to use cat flap as a door and not just as a window.
Stop seeing mice as threatening, but instead recognise them as
   prey.

An Exceptionally Normal Start

Tuesday 1 January

1st 4lb (but winter coat), vomited 3 times (but effectively
covered 4 chairs), caught fire 0 times (excellent).

0500	Got up – woke household.
0502	Went back to bed.
0800	Got up for breakfast of Duck and Rabbit Jellied Catfood (ugh) and Felix Senior Cat Biscuits (v.g.).
0805	Went to bed.
1545	Got up, went out and did something totally demented. Had bad accident. Very lucky this time.
1600	Went to bed.
1755	Jumped onto porch roof to watch out for baby and other two to arrive home in car as required feeding.
1756	Had bad fall from porch roof. Nobody saw (phew!).
1758	Baby and other two arrived home. Boy delivering leaflets *did* see and explained in alarmed way about my falling off roof. They talked to him in soothing tones.
1800	Ran to greet them in drive. The baby clumped me with her plastic mallet (quite hard).
1805	Ate dinner. Sheba Gold (excellent).
1810	Went to bed.

1825 Sheba Gold not so good on way out. Baby evacuated and area coated in 'Pet Accident' foam spray. Moved to another bed.

1830 (Thoughts) If I can stick to my no-smoking policy and keep vomiting down to present levels, the white cat may very well begin seeing me in a different light.

1910 As 1825.

1930 As 1910.

Wednesday 2 January

0800 Caught fire.

Batman in White Ankle Socks

'Far hence, keep far from me, you grim woman.'

Ovid

When I were just a lad my parents had two cats.
Penny, a tortoiseshell, was a nice, friendly, shy sort of cat. She went through life without having any books written about her, kept herself to herself, you know the sort.

Cindy, her younger housemate, was pure undiluted evil.

She'd have looked evil too, if it hadn't been for her feet. She was mainly jet black. The bottom half of her face, from just below her nose, was white. And so were all four paws. This made her look for all the world as if she were wearing a black mask and white socks. She looked like Batman. Batman in white ankle socks.

Cindy was scheming, nasty, vicious and deadly.

We liked her a lot.

My father believed she was watching him and that she had some dark agenda all of her own. Now Dad may never have been the sharpest tool in the box, but there did seem to be something odd about her relationship with him at that time.

He claimed that he could sense her staring at him, wherever he was, whatever he was doing. We thought he was being paranoid at first.

We'd be sitting at dinner and he would say that he just knew she was somewhere, watching his every move. There'd be no sign of her and we'd laugh at him. And then eventually one of us would spot a small black and white face peering out from a clump of shrubs at the end of the garden. She would be staring straight at Dad through the patio doors. It could send a bit of a shiver down the spine.

Once he was lying and relaxing in the bath with the door

locked. Eyes shut, music on, singing and humming, he opened his eyes to grab the shampoo . . . and almost had a heart attack.

There, sitting on the toilet cistern and grinning straight at him was Cindy. The room had definitely been empty when he'd closed his eyes.

At this point he must have truly believed his own tongue in cheek theories about her (I *hope* they were tongue in cheek).

A little detective work revealed how she had performed this little piece of magic. In the bedroom next door to the bathroom, the net curtains were hanging out through the fanlight. She'd climbed from the bedroom window, walked along the roof to the bathroom window, and squeezed in through that fanlight. The fact that she later began climbing into every bedroom on our terraced block in this manner proved our theory.

So that was how she'd done it, all that needed answering now was *why*.

Surely seeing my father in the bath was an experience most people would have gone out of their way to avoid. The post-traumatic stress counselling alone would have made this a financially ruinous idea. But Cindy actually risked life and limb just to be there, on that cistern, when he opened his eyes.

I have my own theories about why she did it. In many ways I agree with my father. She did indeed have her own reasons for watching him. But I don't think it was down to some dark and evil masterplan.

I think it was a very feline thing she was doing. She knew it wound him up, plagued him and unsettled him so she *had* to do it.

That's what cats do. They will usually sleep where they know you don't want them to, on a newly changed white sheet or on your face. They will always manage to get into the rooms they are expressly forbidden to go into. They will always seek to sit on the lap of the person who doesn't like cats. They seem to sense when something is wrong and then automatically do it.

And so, as unsettling as her behaviour may have seemed, she was just being a cat. However, I am not totally sure that what she did to me when I was about eighteen was either natural or normal. Better explain that, sounds vaguely disturbing.

She executed what I believe to have been a pre-meditated, cold and calculating attack on me at a time when I was virtually unable to defend myself. She left me for dead, bleeding and unconscious in an alleyway.

Pretty heavy stuff, huh?

I will start from the beginning.

From when I was about ten years old, Cindy was a part of my life. I was a fairly normal sort of lad at that age, i.e. horrible.

Most of my games were war games. When Action Man was captured he was hung, as a warning to other Action Men. Little plastic soldiers went down in a hail of elastic bands, stones and water bombs. No quarter was requested and none given. Subbuteo players were summarily executed by toy machine-gun firing squad for losing a home league game to the kid next door.

In summary I was a wicked, nasty little boy, rejoicing in gore and carnage. Normal. One good thing was that I felt no animosity towards my cats, and was not usually cruel to any living creature. One bad thing was that what a ten- or eleven-year-old boy thinks isn't cruel, can actually be quite cruel.

And so it was that Penny tried out an Action Man parachute from my mum's bedroom window, whilst Cindy was taken three miles from home on a pushbike to see whether she got home before another boy's cat who'd suffered exactly the same fate.

In my mind such things weren't cruel. Cats land on their feet, don't they? And as double security, Penny was wearing a parachute. As treble security, she was aimed at the fishpond. So all angles had been covered. The fact that the parachute didn't open and she hit the water with quite considerable force was . . . regrettable. She was fine though, and her second jump was far more successful (she missed the fishpond).

And in Cindy's case, cats can find their way home, can't they?

I thought she'd be home by teatime. Mistakes had been made however. Difficult to memorise a route from inside a zipped-up Watford Football Club sportsbag. When she hadn't come home a few days later, I searched her drop-off zone thoroughly, but with no luck.

I finally told my mother, who took what I'd done very well, putting it down to youthful exuberance. When I was able to sit on the saddle of my pushbike again and Mum had decided not to apply for a care order, I was sent pedalling off with the sportsbag now full of 'LOST CAT' leaflets and sellotape.

When the phone call finally came from a couple who'd managed to corner her and lock her in their shed, she'd been missing for two weeks. She was skinny, dirty, wild-eyed and damn near feral. My mum was so relieved that she forgave me. My sister had far too many issues with me to bother forgiving me for just one, and my dad had never held it against me anyway, taking on a relaxed air about the whole thing and sitting beside windows again. Penny was furious she was back, but not with me.

So that only left Batman, and she would never, ever forgive me.

I was never really her friend in the years following that episode. An incident with one of those aforementioned water bombs did little to get me back in her good books. Neither did an almost nasty accident involving a length of string, two eggs, a fishing net and a small explosive device. For her part, she became understandably vicious towards me. I would have to take all sorts of precautions, such as always shutting the lavatory door. I lost count of the times that Cindy rushed in there, whilst I was 'busy' and bit me hard on the foot or ankle. She would then leave as fast as she'd arrived, with me totally immobilised and unable to give chase. Not unless I wanted to pay the carpet cleaning costs anyway.

I wonder if this toilet terrorism gave her the idea that guerrilla warfare was her ticket to victory. To get in there when my defences (and my trousers) were down, strike, and get the hell out. If she could take her water closet warmongering into the field, she had a chance . . .

By the time I was eighteen, Barbie was infinitely more interesting than Action Man. I don't mean I played with Barbies or hung Barbie as a warning to other Barbies or anything, I just thought they were better to look at, that's all.

Apart from women, the other great interest in my life was beer which I loved like a brother. Beer made all sorts of weird and wonderful things happen, beer made you charming, hilarious and cool, albeit only to yourself and your equally bladdered drinking buddies.

Whilst I pursued the new loves of my life, my little arch enemy, Batman, was watching and waiting. Whether she noticed my inability after midnight to open the front gate or avoid ploughing through my father's flowerbeds, I don't know. Neither do I know whether she realised that there was a pattern to my late-night antics and that I was 100% more likely to walk straight through next door's hedge on a Saturday night than on any other night of the week.

If she *did* know then it would explain why she chose the early hours of that warm Sunday morning to try to kill me.

I have only vague memories of her attack. I'd had one hell of a night and staggered up our path at what must have been about 3.30 in the morning. We had an open alleyway down the side of our house, bordered by a brick wall on one side and our neighbour's shed on the other. As I zigzagged from brick to wood, unbeknown to me, Cindy lay in wait on top of the shed.

Without warning I was attacked from above. A screeching object landed on my head and sunk its claws into my scalp and forehead. I stumbled forward thrashing at thin air, finally colliding with a metal dustbin which for some reason I decided to take with me for a few yards before crashing to the hard concrete pavement, sending empty milk bottles flying into the air. Batman only jumped clear as I hit the ground.

Head on the floor, I remember watching her legging it up the back lawn. I don't remember anything after that.

My mother had heard a great commotion outside in the night, but great commotions had become an accepted norm. When she found me at 8 a.m. I was surrounded by broken glass and the contents of the dustbin, which I seemed to be cuddling. My face was streaked with blood and my knees and hands were bleeding. We didn't know if the food in which my head was resting had come from the bin or me. My right elbow was so badly bruised I could barely straighten my arm for a week. Whether Cindy had returned to defecate on me or if what was on my back was simply from a binned litter tray we shall never know.

Fair enough, I say.

Crackpot Theories

'Hats off gentlemen, a genius!'
Robert Schumann

I've always been fascinated by the concept of a fully evolved domestic cat civilisation.

It took around sixty million years for a strain of the very basic miacis to evolve into the sophisticated felis lybica, or African wildcat, from which all of our domestic cats descend. So where will cats be in another sixty million years, or another two hundred million years?

I once wrote a fantasy/comedy book that involved advanced extra-terrestrial feline astronauts descending upon a sleepy, predominantly inebriated, English village, and needed to consider exactly what the motivations and ambitions of a feline world would be.

For the sake of fun, the cats were bi-pedal, had mastered space travel and were primarily here because they'd exhausted their stocks of small and helpless creatures.

What struck me in the writing of the book, however, was this: could a cat society ever have the drive to become a technological and industrial civilisation, given what we know of their basic character traits at this moment in time?

Probably not. They wouldn't be awake long enough. A cat sleeps for about twenty hours a day, leaving four hours for work, play, eating, etc. We sleep about eight of every twenty-four hours, leaving sixteen hours for work and play.

So, we are awake around 5,840 hours per year, a cat for only 1,460 hours. Over the course of a hundred years, we have 438,000 more waking hours than a cat, meaning that, per century, a human being is awake fifty years longer than a cat. Over the course of a millennium of potential progress, a cat would be snoring for 833 years out of a thousand. That really doesn't leave much time to get things done, but maybe they'd just get things done on a slower timescale.

So let's assume that they could do it, it would just take a heck of a lot longer. Who'd be in charge? They don't seem too fond of taking orders, do they? Or being trained in any way. They just want to swan along and do things their own way. Rules are pointless. Any instruction not to do a particular thing is taken purely as an added incentive to do it.

Perhaps they could work on a kind of reverse psychology basis, ordering the workforce not to get the next shipment out on time under any circumstances. But, in all truth, you'd never get them to stay at work all day anyway, no matter how comfortable you made it for them. A cat will stay on a cushion all day, until it realises that's where you'd like it to sleep. Then the cushion's off limits. Supervisors could try ordering the workforce not to turn up for work, and then keep telling them to go home all day, but surely a ploy of that nature would soon be sussed out.

I really can't see cats forming a society in which they have to take orders from anyone, so I assume they'd be a race of entrepreneurs. But even then, if a customer tried to buy an item from a tabby cornershop, the shopkeeper would presumably just look at the punter blankly and start washing his arse (actually, that isn't a lot different from the behaviour of many uninterested shop assistants in our own high streets nowadays).

Talking of evolution and shopping in one sentence is fairly unusual and has reminded me of a website I came across while accessing a feline evolutionary chart. The list brought up by my keyword search included a US shopping site offering the remarkable 'Feline Evolution Toilet Seat' at just $112.00, available in salmon, blue or white. I had to know what this thing was immediately.

It proved to be a toilet seat, strangely enough. The catalogue entry confirmed its name and showed a tortoiseshell cat sitting on a standard low-level flush WC with salmon seat, presumably the Feline Evolution Toilet Seat. Beneath it was the caption, 'Save money and enjoy the convenience of not maintaining a litter box for your cat. The Feline Evolution Toilet Seat is guaranteed for virtually any cat.'

And that was it, no further explanation at all. A toilet seat for cats? Guaranteed for virtually *any* cat? What sort of cats do they have over there for pity's sake? It just looked like a normal toilet seat, I squinted at the screen but could see no major difference that would make a cat want to sit above a water-filled hole any more than they would normally want to. I shall have to remain perplexed by this thing, but can only surmise that American cats are already far ahead of our own in the evolutionary stakes.

Where were we? Ah yes . . . the only way forward I can see for a feline industrial revolution is if they had somebody to do it for them. Trained monkeys. Like us. Why not, we do everything for them now. So let's say that whilst the cats are evolving, the human race is regressing.

And there is nothing to suggest that this scenario is not entirely possible. For instance, the Scottish have recently gone through the process of devolution, so although that means something completely different but sounds a lot like the sort of word we want, we will assume that the Scottish are now gradually devolving into a primitive apelike form.

If cats of the future could capture some of these fully devolved Scots and train them to turn the wheels of industry, then suddenly we can see a way forward for feline civilisation.

Getting the Scots captured in the first place should be no problem at all, as one thing that cats do tend to enjoy is hunting. Like us, they hunt for fun. What a terrible pairing we make, cats and humans, sitting smugly in our brick houses, vicious smiling killers in a world where everybody else kills only for territory, status or food (or because they're in a bad mood). The rest of the animal world must look down upon our two species as deeply barbaric and uncultured, in much the same way continental Europeans view the English.

Once the cats have trained their incarcerated Scots to build great cities and man their factories for them, they can settle back into a life of decadence and leisure. They'd really excel at that.

Decadence and leisure is what cats do best. I can see them now. Their days would be spent draped out on piles of silk cushions, clad in togas, being hand-fed spiced mice by delectable Scottish maidens, while canine jesters provide entertainment with silly beg and bark dance routines.

At night the cats would frequent lavish and foppish night-clubs, where pigeons would fly in huge iron cages suspended from the ceilings and mice would run around the cats' heads inside an elaborate system of tangled plastic tubing. All of these nightspots would be excessively classy and sophisticated, except in one detail, the provision of pub spittoons, not seen since the mid-twentieth century, to cater for the age-old habit of furball regurgitation.

Technological innovation would centre around new and ingenious weaponry for hunting and killing, the feline way. Smart bullets would fly at their victim, stop, toy with him, cuff him around a bit and then drag him home and leave him on the doorstep.

Genetics would centre on the creation of flightless birds, three-legged mice, jumping fish and non-biting fleas with combs for hands. Dolly, the self-replicating vole with a delicate rainbow trout aftertaste, would become a household name.

Would there be a space industry?

Of course. Cats are renowned for their curiosity, and if curiosity is going to kill the cat, what better way for it to do so than by propelling him into orbit atop three thousand gallons of ignited rocket fuel.

They would *have* to go into space. Cats would just have to know what's 'out there'. They couldn't tolerate not knowing.

With the aid of their short-sleeping Scottish workforce they would conquer the universe in an incredibly short time, pushing outwards, always outwards, into the great unknown.

And what of religion? Would cats evolve worshipping gods? I can't see it somehow. Cats don't worship. They expect to be worshipped. I would imagine that laws would be passed decreeing that cats *are* gods.

If they become the gods, would there be a devil? Maybe they would delve into the murky past of race history and call their devil Schrödinger.

Schrödinger, their traditions would tell, wanted all cats' souls, and when he got them he would lock them away in boxes.

In the boxes, the tormented cats would be both alive and dead at the same time, and would never know which unless Schrödinger opened the box. Cat mothers would tell their kittens that if they didn't behave, then Schrödinger would get them and put them in a box: 'Be good now, because you wouldn't want to be Schrödinger's cat now, would you?'

Incidentally, if you aren't familiar with the name Schrödinger, he was an Austrian scientist who won a Nobel Prize for his work in the field of physics. A famous theory of his became known as Schrödinger's Cat. The idea of Schrödinger's Cat was to explain the theory of quantum physics by putting a cat into a box with a vial of poison and a radioactive atom. If the atom decayed it would break the vial and release the poison, thus killing the cat. If the vial remained intact, the cat would live. Whilst the cat was inside, the onlooker wouldn't know which scenario existed within the box, and therefore both did. The cat was both alive and dead at the same time, and so therefore sub-atomic particles can exist in different states at the same time.

Which if you don't mind me saying so, sounds like a right load of old bollocks. The cat's dead or it's not, isn't it? Whether the onlooker knows or not is surely irrelevant. I realise I am being grossly simplistic here and entirely missing the point, but whether the theory was proved or disproved by this experiment, it would do little to endear him to any cats who might hear about it.

Would there be wars? Whilst lions may fight in packs, this is a domestic cat world we're imagining, and they tend to go it alone, so I don't think organised warfare would be a major problem.

Judging by their normal attitudes to fighting, any war would take far too long to ever get started. A one-on-one scrap gener-ally takes for ever to get off the ground, so I'd say that at least a thousand-year stand-off would have to be expected as a precursor to any major international conflict.

So there we have it. The feline utopia of the year Sixty Million AD.

And what would Brum's descendants' part be in this brave new world?

Would the sons of Brum take their rightful place amongst the planet's new elite? Would they live a life of luxury and have Feline Evolution Toilet Seats?

Would they heck . . . they'd all be Scottish by then.

A Fate Worse Than Fireworks

'As he rose like the rocket,
he fell like the stick.'

Thomas Paine

Brum's bonfire night that first year at Lorraine's was his worst ever, and not for the reasons you'd probably assume. His problems that night had nothing to do with Roman candles, kids with bangers or air bomb repeaters. Strangely, neither did he fall asleep inside a Guy or blunder into a bonfire. A launching rocket, about to take off and roar 300 feet above a field before exploding into a fiery kaleidoscope didn't lodge in his collar and take him with it. Sparks returning to ground didn't ignite his fur and add another episode in his long history of fire-related accidents.

No, the reason he had such a terrible night was much more unusual.

Sammy sat on his head all night.

Before I go further into this terrible story, the sparks returning to ground thing was more a case of personal memory than a made-up scenario. Years ago I was at an organised fireworks display at our local cricket club.

On that particular night, either because of a miscalculation or high winds, I can't remember which, quite a few burning embers missed their fall-out zone and landed amongst the crowd. It was nothing major and added to the excitement more than anything else.

However, it did cause a few problems. My friend got some hot ash in his eye, for instance, and ended up needing treatment. A man in front of me had his coat catch fire. I also needed treatment because I got decked by the man whose coat was on fire.

With hindsight, I should have told him what I was doing when I saw his back start to smoulder and not just dance about and start slapping him like Julian Clary in a prize fight.

As he turned round and walloped me he must have truly believed that he was defending himself from an unprovoked attack from some dangerous nutter setting about innocent people (albeit in a girly-hitting way) at firework displays. He probably still believes that to this day. He'd gone by the time I got up.

Anyway, Sammy sitting on Brum's head.

Brum may have found a new home, but it was still very much Sammy's house. Brum knew his place and that was as Sammy's barely tolerated guest.

Sammy had strict house rules for guests:

1. Keep out of my way or you will die.
2. Touch my food and you will die.
3. Do not lie on my chair or on my bed or you will die. For clarification, all of the chairs and all of the beds are mine.
4. If you use any of my private hiding places and cubby holes you will definitely die, possibly more than once.
5. Everywhere else in the house is also mine. You will know if I am not happy about where you are sitting because you will die.
6. You may die anyway.

The rules were clear for the most part, but rule four seems to have slipped his mind on fireworks night.

Funnily enough, Brum has always had a huge respect for fireworks. Whereas he will court danger in most walks of life, fireworks night has always been 'helmets on and down to the shelters' for him.

At my old flat, he always used to spend the night in the bathroom. Not because he was nervous and we'd got a Feline Evolution Toilet Seat or anything, but because the room was small and had no windows and undoubtedly felt secure.

But, this being his first bonfire night in his new home, he hadn't given a new hiding place much thought when the first window-rattling explosions started going off.

For ten minutes he raced around the place frantically. Finally he was gone and we had no idea where. The cat flap was locked with both he and Sammy safely inside, so he couldn't have got out. We assumed he must be well hidden somewhere or other and forgot about him.

Sammy's no fan of fireworks either. She has her own bunker, just as Brum had his at the flat. Hers is behind a chest of drawers in the bedroom. The small recess behind the drawers is only about the same size as she is. To get into the recess, she has to jump on to a wooden box to the side of them and then drop over into the very cramped space behind.

All evening long the pops and bangs went off outside, and Sammy's wide eyes were visible, peering worriedly from her dark hiding place.

At eleven o'clock we were about to go to bed when I realised that I still hadn't seen any sign of Brum. By that time of night you'd normally have been aware of him at some point, whether through the distant breaking of china in a back room or the thump of falling tabby on lino in the kitchen.

I called his name (he usually comes running or at least meows back – he's very polite).

I heard his distinct voice calling back to me, very close but muffled. He sounded distressed. I called again, and again heard his meow. It seemed to be coming from Sammy.

Lorraine thought so too. I called one more time and we both stared at Sammy. The meow came directly from her but her lips didn't move. Either she'd taken up ventriloquism and mimicry or Brum was extremely close to her. For one mad moment, the self-satisfied look on Sammy's face and Brum's muffled meows emanating from her convinced me she'd eaten him.

Lorraine walked over to Sammy and lifted her out of the recess, something I wouldn't have even attempted doing for fear of never being able to use a keyboard again. The removal of Sam's weighty mass revealed a severely shocked tabby.

Little can he have imagined when he chose that hiding place the horrors that the night had in store. I wonder if Sammy even knew she was sitting on him. She may have just found it a bit warmer and softer in there than usual.

When you think about it, what a terrible experience.

The fireworks are really bothering him, when a cat he's terrified of comes and sits on him. Not only is he trapped in a tiny dark hole with explosions going off all around, he's too scared to move a muscle for four hours lest the vicious killer cat sitting on his head detects his presence.

Worse still, Sammy was only in there, her rear end in his face, because she was also terrified by the fireworks. A human in the same situation, cowering under cover from an earsplitting airborne attack, would definitely have required the odd change of underwear during the course of the evening.

I find the picture too horrible to continue painting.

It's a Knockout!

'*We are all of us in the gutter, but some of us are looking at the stars.*'

Oscar Wilde

If Brum could understand me, the first thing I'd tell him to do would be to consider investing in a good medical plan. Also, I would explain to him that the old nine lives policy upon which he currently relies is almost definitely about to expire.

The first intelligent contact between Human and Feline could really be a little more earth-shattering and memorable than that, couldn't it?

Scholars would no doubt later comment that 'We offer peace and goodwill to your kind . . . Tiddles,' would have made better historical script than 'Are you sorted for insurance mate?'

But that and a frank health and safety discussion it should be for he and I. It's what he needs most in the world. As I may have mentioned in passing, Brum is a catastrophically clumsy creature. Coming as he does from a species that oozes cool style and agility, his lack of coordination is all the more noticeable. In fairness of course, had he been born into a different species he'd probably have never carried out any of the crazy acrobatics that cause accidents in the first place.

Crazy acrobatics are very much a cat thing. Many species simply aren't capable of even attempting them. Take me for example, a human being (loosely speaking). Imagine all fourteen stone of me prancing across the rooftops, deftly sending tiles and guttering crashing to the ground as I majestically launch headfirst towards a ridiculously thin fence ten feet below. Arms stretched forward for landing, one broken wrist shoots right, the other left as my face hits wood with a splintering thump. My legs choose much the same course and my chances of a larger family suffer a blindingly painful setback.

As I keel gracelessly sideways and head for the ground, there is just time to destroy the garden furniture on the way down. I bounce twice before finally becoming stilled, a groaning lump in the middle of the patio.

Fortunately I rarely do things like that. But of course, Brum has to. Unfortunately, his execution is much the same as mine. Seemingly impossible I know, but then Brum has shown me many things that seemed impossible before he actually did them. None of them nice.

For instance, it's apparently very rare to see a cat knocked out. Our vet* has confirmed this. Unconscious following a serious accident, yes. Out for the count after a smack in the face, no. And yet Brum achieves oblivion quite easily. The first time (to my knowledge – I presume he must be doing these things when I'm *not* around) was in the kitchen.

Brum's least endearing habit is his jumping onto kitchen work surfaces. Peaceful negotiation (*'Get down!'*) and military action (pushing him off) have failed to break this habit. After a lifetime of bouncing straight back onto the worktops like some tabby Tigger he now no doubt considers this his job and, not wanting to interfere with his livelihood, I've largely given up the fight.

However, when we're preparing food, the old 'push and bounce' routine comes back into play. During this particular minced beef cremation, Brum had accomplished many footholds on easily reached surfaces only to be pushed to ground immediately. Distinctly peeved with the situation, he decided to approach from a different, and infinitely more difficult, angle.

He chose a route awash with peril – sharp knives, plates, pots and pans, open cupboards and drawers and, most significantly, a tray hanging over the edge of the work surface.

I saw him launch upwards out of the corner of my eye. All

---

* Our vet has a twitching eye. I have no idea if this only occurs when he's around Brum. His entire attitude to Brum reminds me very much of Herbert Lom's towards Inspector Clouseau in the *Pink Panther* movies – the same manic tic, the same contemptuous, wild-eyed glare – so I do tend to favour the theory that his seeing Brum and I brings on a spontaneous nervous attack.

four paws landed firmly on the tray. Objective achieved? No. The tray began rocking in a wild see-saw motion before tipping backwards over the edge. Brum's frantic disembarkation attempt achieved three things – firstly he spilt a full jug of water over his head, secondly – the jug smacked him between the ears, and thirdly – he didn't actually get off the tray. The front half made it but his backside was already on the way down. The result was a cringe-inducing smack to the jaw, formica to tabby.

As the tray and various items of cutlery crashed to the floor around him, I have to admit that he himself slid to the floor with an easy grace he could never have hoped to have achieved had he been conscious. I automatically assumed him dead, shrugged and carried on with the cooking. No, not really – I automatically assumed him dead and rushed to his side, very nearly kicking a grounded bread knife into him and finishing the job. By the time I knelt down among the debris his eyes flicked open, and they continued to open until they were wide, staring shocked pools. He looked at me in wonder and bit me.

Not many weeks later, Brum sat staring at a cat-flap. Not long installed back then, this thing was a source of amazement to Brum, but of no practical use whatsoever. Not so for Brum's live-in-partner-girl-cat Sammy, who loved her new-found freedom, so much so that she actually bothered to get out of bed and clatter back and forth into the early hours of the morning.

Now, Sammy may be a nice-looking girl but she's quite a large and heavy beast. She also flies through the cat-flap with totally unnecessary force, as if trying to punch a hole in the door with her head. And, fairly predictably, she chose that very moment on a Saturday afternoon, with Brum making the transition from staring aghast at the cat-flap to tentatively sniffing it, to come hurtling through from the other side like a guided missile.

Brum was hammered squarely under the chin by eighteen pounds of ballistic cat and metal with such force that he rose a foot in the air. Staggering backwards on his hind legs like a cabaret dancing dog, his eyes rolled upwards and he slumped to the floor. Sammy, affronted by his sudden appearance in her flight path, became a white and brown blur of teeth and claws as she launched a pointless offensive against an opponent whose lights were well and truly out.

Giving up in the face of no resistance, she offered him only a cursory backward glance as she trotted back off to bed, avoiding the legs of helpers rushing to Brum's aid. He came-to in much the same way as the first time round and resumed his cat-flap vigil. I somehow avoided the temptation to knock him back out and went to find myself a plaster.

A little later he pushed his head through the cat-flap. Much later his front paws followed. His forward half remained outside, his rear end poking, a little unnervingly, back into the hallway. Much, much later it began to rain. Hard.

Have you ever seen a long-haired cat drenched from head to belly, and fluffy and dry from belly to tail? A viewing is highly recommended . . . looks very much like half a poodle.

The Babysitter

'Thou Art the Man!'
II Samuel Chapter 12 Verse 7

B rum is a warm and loving cat by nature. The old adage of the cats with the worst breath usually being the friendliest is completely true. But he is only this way with people.

He is not at all fond of most other cats. That may just be a jealousy thing. As with all cats, he can safely look down at the human race, seeing us as providers and taking us for mugs. But he must see other cats in much the same way I'd imagine a chimpanzee sees a human being or, for that matter, a miacis sees a cat, i.e. 'They look a lot like me, but they seem a hell of a lot smarter.'

Brum's levels of warmth and pity for mankind reached new heights upon the birth of our daughter Maya. We were warned many times during Lorraine's pregnancy that cats were dodgy and dangerous around babies. We were told terrible stories of cats lying on babies in the night and smothering them, of vicious scarring and jealousy. Brum and hard-as-nails Sammy were therefore eyed with deep suspicion for nine months.

For their part they acted with just a little too much nonchalant disinterest for our liking. Apart from shocked faces each morning at the horrendous gagging sounds emanating from the bathroom, they showed nothing. Poker faced. Holding their cards close to their chests. But we knew what they were capable of. We were on to them.

When Maya arrived, they were fascinated in a horrified kind of way. They spent many hours staring but never ventured close. This may have been purely down to the threatening looks from Maya's paranoid and utterly out-of-depth parents. What was very heartening however was that neither showed any signs of aggression.

And then Maya showed them the good life. The house no

longer slept at night. It was New York and Ibiza all rolled into one. There were bright lights, there was screaming, there was rocking and singing. They found that food was available at three in the morning and they could watch TV until dawn. This weird-looking little alien had transformed their lives and they idolised her for it.

If Maya cried they were there for her. Brum would stand at her bedroom door with a worried expression while Sammy would go for help. Consequently we awoke groggily to piercing baby shrieks only to have the wind knocked from our bodies by a frantic cat landing on our stomachs.

I envision this whole thing as a scene from ER. As one of us 'doctors' makes our way down the corridor to Maya's room, Sammy runs busily alongside, the worried orderly, filling us in on exactly what has happened. Brum is there to meet us at the door and hand us the patient's file. Both concerned and solemn order-lies stare into the room as the doctor attends to the howling patient. And then the orderlies want feeding.

The cats' attitude to Maya came as a bit of a relief. Far from becoming baby-hating vengeful monsters, they seemed to actu-ally like her. This affection became more apparent in Brum as Maya got older. Whilst Sammy drifted back to normality after a few months, Brum got closer to Maya. Much too close in fact. Close enough for Maya to perpetrate indignities and unpleas-antries upon him that I will not describe here as this is supposed to be a nice, warm chapter. Let's just say that given what he went through in her first year, his affection was all the more surprising.

Now, whilst we were grateful for once to our feline friends for making life a little easier, we couldn't, in our wildest dreams, have anticipated what was to happen next.

Some things in life are very strange indeed. Brum has taken his relationship with Maya to a stage that all hassled parents would willingly pay him for. He has become her babysitter.

Social Services will be on their way right now, so I need to explain that a little. We don't tend to go out and leave our sixteen-month-old child in the hands of a cat who has attained levels of incompetence inconceivable even for a feline, never mind in the field of childcare.

Not often anyway, if at all.

Those with a baby should be very familiar with this particular scene of domestic bliss. Your child is in her cot. You've stroked her head and hummed inanely for most of the last hour. She finally falls asleep. You leave her door ajar as the click could wake her from her early stages of slumber. You grab a beer, put your feet up and settle down to watch the movie and . . . WAAAAAAAAHHHHHHHH!

The next bit you may not be so familiar with.

Your sleeping tabby raises his head from the rug by the fire, and stretches in a resigned, fed up sort of way, as if the baby's crying is somehow his problem and he must deal with it. He slopes off out of the room without so much as a glance in your direction and heads off for your baby's room.

Your baby stops crying. There is some chatter as she welcomes your tabby to her cot-side. The tabby remains at the bars of her cot until she is sleeping peacefully once more. He then wanders back into the sitting room, head down, and slumps back onto the rug as if nothing has happened. If she wakes a little later, he will do it all again.

This is all absolutely true. We couldn't believe it either.

The first time he did it, I naturally went with him. I stood at the door and watched as he stared through the bars at Maya. Maya relaxed instantly and cooed and chuckled at him. He moved not an inch, just stood and stared. Occasionally a little hand would take a swipe at his head and he had to jerk back out of harm's reach. But he didn't leave until she was asleep.

How much can that be worth? A free tabby babysitting service?

He doesn't always do it, but he does it often enough to make a huge difference to our evenings. Enough in fact, that when we hear Maya's howl all eyes in the room, even Sammy's, turn automatically to Brum.

The only time he won't do it is during the early hours of the morning . . . and we do need to work on that.

Baby Trouble

I like Little Pussy, her coat is so warm,
And if I don't hurt her she'll do me no harm;
So I'll not pull her tail, nor drive her away,
But pussy and I very gently will play.

Mother Goose, circa 1760

I marvel sometimes at Brum's patience.

The physical and mental abuse he receives and calmly absorbs at the hands of Baby Maya is quite breathtaking. It's not as if he needs to either.

He is roughly the same size as her and their weights aren't much different, which from Maya's perspective, makes him the equivalent of a Bengal tiger. If Maya really understood what she was dealing with, she wouldn't go near him with any less than a whip, a stool and a couple of armed gamekeepers.

In short, he could have her over, no problem. But she really doesn't understand that, and Brum's good nature and lack of reasoning virtually rule out the possibility that he would have ever weighed up the odds.

And so it is that the balance of power lies with the baby and not the sitter. Unfortunately, like so many other despots in history, a little power has gone to her head and she has grossly abused it.

We try to protect Brum from her, obviously. But with Maya, as with most things in his life, he sets himself up for the fall, and there is often little we can do to help him. He takes the knocks and just keeps bouncing back for more. And more.

His first real interaction with Maya should have been warning enough. Alarm bells should have been ringing through the thick fog of his mind. But that fog seems all-consuming and even sound is lost in its dense grey blanket. His first little tentative sniff at Maya was greeted by a hard punch on the nose. His reaction was to lean back in goggle-eyed amazement. And then sniff her again . . . and get punched again. We had to pull him away. I think he would have gone into a permanent sniff and punch cycle had we not broken his momentum.

Thus started a relationship which has changed very little over the past sixteen months. It's not that Maya doesn't like Brum. She really does. Half of what she does to him is out of sheer lack of coordination. The other half is out of a baby's natural ability to find great humour in inflicting pain and punishment on those they love without guilt or remorse.

From the word go, Maya could not understand the concept of stroking a cat. We tried to teach her gradually by demonstrating whilst crooning ooos and ahhhs. She would manage a couple of strokes, and then slap him round the face and punch him in the kidneys, which to her mind obviously seemed a much better idea.

On one memorable occasion, she was stroking Brum quite nicely while he sat on the infamous kitchen work surface. I was holding her in my arms and keeping a close eye on the situation. Her hand was buried in his long fur and she was trying out the ooo and ahhh sounds. Then things went pear shaped.

The phone rang and I started heading for the hall. As myself and Maya departed there was an almighty crash behind us. I turned to see Brum staggering groggily out of the open dishwasher that had been immediately below him. A plate was in two pieces and Brum had a generous splattering of tomato sauce across his face.

I stared in wonder for a few seconds and then just couldn't help myself. By the time I answered the phone I was incoherent with laughter and tears were rolling down my cheeks. It was a market researcher if I recall correctly, who by my gasps and howls must have truly believed that either a dog had answered the phone or he'd called some kind of 'dial a pervert' chat line.

As with so many Brum mishaps, it was the sheer absurdity of the incident that had appealed to my sense of humour. How on earth had he managed to simply drop like a stone straight into the dishwasher as we walked away?

It was a couple of minutes later, while putting the phone down on the bewildered researcher who had valiantly attempted to carry on while no doubt feeling threatened, and possibly used, that I got my clue.

Clutched in my daughter's little left hand was a great clump of tabby fur. What must have happened hit me, and I admit shamefully, reduced me to tears of laughter once again.

Maya had grabbed the fur she was stroking as I walked away, hauling Brum bodily from the work surface and never loosening that fierce monkeylike grip even as he bade a sad farewell to his fur and hurtled rear first into the dishwasher.

Maya pulling his fur became a bit of a problem after that. She found that Brum would come down off the sofa much faster if hauled by fur and ears. The long-suffering Brum didn't seem to mind at all. He would shoot me a worried glance now and then as I remonstrated with Maya about gentleness and other things alien to her, but that was about it.

Her most notable early assault on Brum involved an armed attack with a mallet. This vicious toddling encounter ended with a fall, as do so many things for Brum. It came at the end of a particularly bad week in Maya and Brum's developing relationship. Brum had struck back for the first time, causing massive alarm in Maya's mother. He hadn't used his claws however, and merely dobbed her on the arm after she tried to wrench his collar over his head and half choked him. As usual the speed and suddenness of her attack prevented me from intervening in time to stop it. I chastised Brum with a few sharp words for 'going for her' which made me feel pretty bad as he'd put up with an awful lot and, I'm convinced, intended his swipe only as a warning. Brum was, quite rightly, deeply offended by this and started sitting in a back room and ignoring Maya altogether.

On the day of the mallet attack, it appeared he'd decided to forgive and forget. He raced down to greet us as we arrived home in the car and then rushed back to position himself on the lower part of our front wall, so that he'd be face to face with us as we reached the top of the steps.

It seemed at first that Maya was delighted he'd seen sense and come over to her way of thinking, i.e. cats are great fun and don't mind being pushed about a bit. Sitting in my arms, she gently stuck her left hand out to him and he brushed his face against it. The feint with the left was to cover the right, which now swung with great force and crashed its little plastic mallet straight into the side of Brum's head. While he was still off balance from the first blow and I was trying to get hold of her mallet, she rabbit-punched him with an outstretched left and threw her head at him in a vicious attempted head-butt.

A startled and totally off-guard Brum took decisive evasive action, i.e. fell off the wall. Lorraine was walking up the steps with a bag of shopping, totally unaware of the explosive violence that had just taken place, and watched as Brum inexplicably plunged down through the air and crashed into the bushes below. She sighed and carried on up the steps as if this sort of thing happened every day, which in truth, it does.

Brum is a forgiving creature and had forgotten about the incident by the next day, either because he understood that Maya was just a little baby and (possibly) meant no harm, or because he *had* actually forgotten, which is the more likely.

Maya tried to provide him with plenty of memory joggers over the next few months and his patience was tremendous as he allowed himself to be systematically poked, slapped and prodded. Also tremendous was the level of stupidity required to nearly always be within Maya's very limited territory and to almost never spot her menacing one m.p.h. crawling approach.

As she found her feet and became able to prop herself up against the furniture, she found that if she pulled on the black and grey tail dangling provocatively from tabletops and cupboards then there would be a loud squawking sound, often followed by a bonus cat crashing to the ground. It had the addictive quality of a one-armed bandit fruit machine.

As time went on, however, the pokes, slaps and prods became hugs, strokes and kisses. Maya began to warm to her big dopey man-eating tiger.

Nowadays she has an obvious affection for him, but this makes his life no easier. Instead of wanting to smack the living daylights out of him, she now wants to carry him and ride him.

The carrying is a bit of a problem. There is no way on earth she can lift Brum by his midriff but she tries anyway, stooping and grabbing him around the waist, grunting like an over-strained weightlifter. It looks ridiculous. His back arches up as she exerts maximum effort, but all four feet stay firmly on the ground. He just stands purring with a dumb look on his face as Maya tries from every angle. But she *has* worked out that she can, in fact, get two legs off the ground by lifting both back paws at once, and that this causes him to move forward in a faltering stumble – a scene that looks uncannily like a baby–cat wheelbarrow racing team about to tumble to the ground.

Her riding him is more of a problem, and here at last, Brum is getting a little piece of revenge for a bad year. When Maya rushes him, hooks both legs over his back and grabs at his neck for support, Brum displays a deftness and agility we had no idea he possessed. He moves like a greased eel and simply slides from beneath her. Maya, leaning forward and suddenly with no support, ends up flat on her face. Indeed, now that she is shakily mobile, many of her dealings with Brum leave her on the deck. It is perhaps little wonder that amongst her first words, alongside mummy, daddy, milk, dummy and nana are *Bad Cat*, delivered with a wagging finger.

Two recent additions to her vocabulary are get and down. These, when spoken with the favourite word cat (she says cat in the same contemptuous way one might say 'scum') make her longest sentence yet and show just how full-time a job it is, for all three of us, to keep Brum off those damn work surfaces.

Interestingly, she doesn't call Brum's live-in-partner-girl-cat Sammy 'Cat'. Sammy is wise enough to always be in a different room from Maya and watches smugly as Brum constantly blunders into his baby troubles. On the rare occasions that Maya catches sight of the rapidly leaving white blur she usually refers to her as Sammy (or words almost like Sammy anyway). We always call Brum by his name and not Cat, but it is only him who's referred to in this condescending manner.

It leads me to wonder if Maya actually sees the swift, agile and graceful Sammy and the lumbering Brum as the same species.

She may well believe them to be two completely different types of animal. That a very young child should immediately spot the differences between Brum and a cat, leaves me repondering my miacis theory. I've made a note to find a good picture of a miacis and put it next to that of a cat and then ask Maya to tell me which one is a Sammy and which one's Cat. I feel sure that Cat won't be a cat.

Despite Maya's frequent belly flops around Brum, it's still him who's coming off worse overall. Whilst happily piling her toys onto an armchair, she started repeating the word 'hat'. She'd been using the word quite a lot in the previous week and knew its meaning, but when I looked at her pile of toys I saw nothing fitting the description 'hat'. I mentioned that there was no hat on the chair and she became quite angry, pointing at her upturned basket and shouting 'HAT, HAT!'

I laughed patronisingly and told her that it wasn't a hat – it was a basket. She then thumped the basket repeatedly screaming 'HAT, HAT, HAT!' At this point a disgruntled tabby face popped up with the basket on its throbbing head.

I apologised to Maya. The basket was indeed a hat. I'd had absolutely no idea that she had buried him alive in thirty toys. She still beats him up, but now beats him up in a more educational way.

Another new skill she's developed is the ability to throw things. This isn't good news for Brum as not only does he now have to worry when Maya is in range, he has to watch out for airborne objects coming without warning and from distance. This has brought out a kind of blitz mentality in him. I don't mean by that that he's started talking in a 'chin up' jolly cockney accent and listening to Vera Lynne on his crystal set, just simply that he watches the skies in a way that he hasn't needed to since the end of the Sparrow War.

It's not all bad however.

A particularly matey thing that they do like to do together is steal Sammy's food. Maya will spend ages stumbling from kitchen to lounge carrying one cat biscuit at a time, always from Sammy's bowl, and putting it in front of Brum on the sofa. He will duti- fully eat each biscuit while Maya whoops with joy, before trundling off to get another. When Brum isn't around, she takes biscuits from Sammy's bowl, again one at a time, and carefully places them in Brum's.

Is this favouritism? Or is she fattening him up for the kill?

I don't know which it is, but he certainly appreciates his wait- ress service and self-filling food bowl. So, things are generally improving for Brum on the Maya front, and I think that as Maya gets a little older she will show him the respect that comes with understanding and intelligence.

Or she'll just work out how to saddle him.

Cat on a Bit o' String

'Save us from our friends.'
Proverb

A new neighbour moved in recently. Considering the impact Brum's tenancy has had on our immediate neighbours, it's not altogether surprising the old one went (probably to a property with its own state-of-the-art glass greenhouse and tabby-air-raid-early-warning-system).

With the new people came a new and interesting cat. Interesting simply for being a 'cat on a bit of string' as Farmer Len would say.

Her name is Poppy and she's a bit of an odd one. She lives completely on her nerves and doesn't get out much (more echoes of our life on the farm). When she does go out she gets totally confused and hopelessly lost and has to be tracked down. Our new neighbour has therefore devised a way to let her out without her wandering too far away.

He keeps her in a cat harness, attached to a long piece of string, attached to a heavy lead weight. It may sound a bit restrictive, but maybe it's for the best. She doesn't seem the brightest candle in the church, bless her, and with a tendency to wander aimlessly and a busy main road just through the trees . . .

Brum is fascinated by her. She's probably closer to his IQ than most other cats but I don't think it's that. Neither do I believe he fancies her. His affections (shunned) seem to be for Sammy alone. No, I think it's her bit of string that fascinates him, the simpleton.

His own one-off excursion excepted, I don't think he's ever seen a cat on a bit of string before. I expect he realises that she can't chase him either. Whether or not the bit of string is the reason for his staring I don't know, but he does spend an incredible amount of time watching her. He will sit on top of his twenty-foot wall and gaze down at her for hours.

Mowing the lawn and watching him one afternoon, it got me to thinking: what would happen to Brum if he had to wear one of those things? The whole range of terrible accidents came into my mind as clear as if I was standing there, watching them happen . . .

(Mist clears) . . . Brum is sitting outside our front door. To his left are the steps down to the road, to his right is the twenty-feet drop to next door's drive. But he can't go all the way down the steps as he is attached to a lead weight via a bit of string attached to a harness. His chief persecutor, the baby Maya, appears muttering and stumbling at the top of the steps, her parents close behind her. Before they can stop her she's run towards him shrieking 'Cat!'

In a flash she's picked up his lead weight and hurled it over the wall. Brum and his humans stand frozen in horror as the string unfurls and starts flying over the wall after it. Brum is suddenly wrenched bodily from the ground and hauled back-wards over the wall at incredible speed. There's a huge crash as both he and the lead weight go through a car roof, finishing a job he started two years ago.

Or:

He can't get down the steps, but he can reach the rail fence just the other side of the top step, so he heads for that. He goes under it but can get no further so comes back on the other side of the fence post. He sees a bit of string, just like his, going into next door's garden at exactly the point he went in. Was he being followed?

He carefully follows the string, round and round the fence post until lassoed to it and totally unable to move, almost garrotting himself as he tightens the bonds in his attempts to pull free.

His humans arrive home and he strains sideways, barely able to move his head to see the one called Chris running up the steps, his face obscured by an armful of shopping.

The one called Chris doesn't see the length of string stretching across the steps, held taut by fence and lead weight. Brum feels the string pull harder as the one called Chris trips over it and crashes to the floor, groceries flying everywhere. The fence is uprooted and the pressure on Brum's throat eases slightly. He just has time to see Chris shouting loudly at him before the lead weight flying straight at the back of Chris's head connects and sends Chris face first back into his shopping. The baby is laughing.

Or it could be a positive thing:

He can't go down the steps, so he jumps onto the wall. His accuracy, as usual, is abysmal. Clearing the wall by over two feet, he plummets towards the ground, when, TWANG, he is abruptly stopped in midair, secured to the top by the lead weight. He has become the first self-propelled feline bungee jumper. His people aren't home for another two hours so he is left dangling idly in the breeze until a helpful neighbour alerts the RSPCA to the terrible thing the people at number twenty are doing to their cat.

On our return home we are arrested and ask that the monkey incident and the unfortunate episode with the wallabies be taken into consideration (the positive bit was that he wasn't killed).

Oh, and the bit about monkey cruelty and wallaby problems – it's a fantasy scenario, remember, although I would like to point out here that I don't fantasise about beating up monkeys . . . often.

The Shadow Cat

*'Keep your face to the sunshine and
you cannot see the shadows.'*

Helen Keller

I once saw the shadow of a large cat, but there was no cat.

This was particularly worrying at the time, as I was on holiday in the Lake District and reading a book on the folklore and ghosts of the area. This book told of a mythical large, shadowy, black cat whose appearance was an omen of death. Cheery little bit of holiday reading, but then the dark and threatening mountains of the Lake District are a cheery place to go for your summer holidays.

What really annoyed me was that I was going up a mountain the next day, and an ancient portent of doom suddenly appearing to me was *not* a confidence booster. I survived the mountain, although it was touch and go in the fog up there for a while, but just what was this thing?

As with many mythical creatures and phantoms, it seems to have been conjured by the consumption of a large quantity of alcohol. The fact that I'd had far too many pints of 'Oatmeal Stout' and had read about the creature only two nights previously, I admit could slightly have impaired my judgement. It could also be argued that my reliable witness credibility rating would be a little below zero.

The press would really jump on 'MAN SEES SHADOW OF CAT AFTER HEAVY DRINKING SESSION – BELIEVES IT TO BE MYTHICAL BEAST FROM BOOK HE'S READING' wouldn't they? Probably not.

What keeps this story alive, however, is that I was with three other people, two of whom were also ratted and also saw it. The other was sober and didn't but that doesn't matter (much). What matters is that the others who *did* see it hadn't read the book and knew nothing about the creature.

It was the shadow of a cat moving along the grass at the edge of a dark field alongside us to our left. All lighting came from buildings to our right. We saw the shadow for a good few minutes, the unmistakable outline of a cat. It looked big and looked to be walking with us. Only it definitely wasn't. Try as we might, we could see no cat, just its shadow. And then it was gone.

The reason I mention all this is that I have always liked a good ghost story, and I must admit that I find the ones involving animals (or echoes of giggling children) the spookiest. This subject is particularly relevant as Brum's brother Lester's ghost is believed to have appeared to my niece Emily shortly after his death. Lester was a lovely cat. He belonged to my sister, Sarah, and is the reason that Brum got his name.

All Sarah's cats have been named after places she's visited, hence Paris and Camber. When she named Brum's brother Lester (Leicester) I felt Brum should also be named after a Midlands city, just as a mickey take. So you could say I was taking the piss when I named him Birmingham. He certainly thinks so. Thus the tradition of place names in Brum's family continued, and carries on to this day. Sarah has just named her latest cat Leon, named after Leigh-on-Sea believe it or not.

Sarah was heavily pregnant with Emily when Lester was knocked down by a car outside their home. They buried him in his favourite spot in the garden and gave him a little plaque with the inscription:

> Here he lies
> Amongst the flowers
> And only counts
> The sunny hours
> For him dull days
> Just don't exist
> The brazen-faced old optimist

It was all very sad. He was young when he died and my sister had few photos of him, certainly none on display.

When Emily was about two and a half years old, Sarah mentioned Lester in passing. Emily overheard and said that she really liked Lester. Sarah told her that she hadn't known him. Emily protested that she had, and proceeded to give an uncannily accurate description of his fairly unusual looks.

Sarah's not fond of mysteries and always finds them a little unsettling. She wanted to get to the bottom of this one and probed for more answers. Thinking that Emily must have seen a photo somehow, she pressed for detail as to where exactly he'd been when she saw him.

Emily's answer sent shivers down her spine: 'He came into your tummy when I was in there Mummy.'

Sarah wishes she hadn't asked, but I think it was quite a nice thing for him to have done. I reckon the accident had just that minute happened and he nipped in to say hello before he left. And that's just as likely absolute nonsense.

Emily seemed very receptive to this sort of thing as a child. A week or two later she upset her mum again. Sarah was in the kitchen when Emily called from the living room to tell her that 'the white-haired lady with one eye' was with her again. Sarah's blood froze at the words and she didn't know what to expect as she rushed into the room. Emily was happily pointing to a point just below the ceiling in the corner of the room, claiming that the lady was very nice and often visited her.

If someone was really up there, it was almost certainly my grandmother, Emily's great-grandmother. She lost an eye very near the end of her life and died when Emily was only four months old.

On my sister's last visit to see her in hospital, the doctors refused to let Emily onto the ward as my gran, and many other patients, had chest infections. My gran had dearly wanted to see her little great-granddaughter that day and cried when she realised she wouldn't be allowed to. She never did see Emily again. She died three days later.

My gran was a strong-willed woman, however, and wasn't about to let a minor inconvenience like her own death stop her seeing her great-granddaughter. It sounds very much as though she got her way in the end. She usually did!

I believe Emily to be a fairly reliable witness but her mother, bless her, is not. If others hadn't heard these two stories from Emily herself, I'd have doubted their authenticity.

When it comes to the paranormal, Sarah is one of those who is wary and mistrustful of her own shadow. Her most incredible claim was that a cat she had many years ago could talk. She claimed that, late at night, he would pine for his old owner and call out his name. He would also ask to be let out. Not just by scratching at the door, you understand. No, he used to walk up to Sarah and actually ask, in perfect English, to be let out.

Allegedly.

Now at this point you would think that my sister was a nutter, wouldn't you? You will even more so in a moment.

Let's take both of these claims and look at them closely.

Firstly, the cat crying out for his ex-owner late at night. Sarah wasn't sure if his ex-owner's name was the name he called. She just assumed it must be.

And the name he called? Malcolm.

Malcolm. What does that sound like? Malcolm . . . ah yes – Meow.

Meow-colm, Meow-colm.

Probably just meowing then, rather than lamenting the long lost Malcolm. The fact he was part Siamese (the cat – not Malcolm) would explain the odd twang to the sound.

And of his flawless grasp of the English language? What words did he use? The exact words were 'Let me out.' Couldn't make it clearer than that. Bright cat.

Again though, I'm detecting a flaw here. Let-me-out, Let-me-out.

Let-meow, let-meow? Hmm.

And did he always go out after asking? Not always, no.

My sister is a lovely girl, but sometimes . . .

I was talking about the Lester/Emily story down the pub one

night, and it prompted a few other ghostly pet stories which I rather liked.

The first is apparently true, but the teller had heard or read about it somewhere and had no idea where. A young lady's cat died and was cremated. She lived alone and had been very sorry to have had to have him put down due to ill health. One night, a few weeks after his death, she sat in her lounge and heard a wailing from outside. It sounded uncannily like her own cat's cry and the noise chilled her to the bone. She looked out of the window but could see nothing. She noted an odd echo-like quality to the wailing, as if it came from a distant, empty room. The following night, she heard the sound again and, although frightened, she walked out into the dark garden, but could see no sign of any cats. Strangely, the sound seemed to be coming from back in the house rather than the garden. She went inside and listened. Again the wailing had an echo, that feeling of an empty room. It seemed to be coming from above. And then, with a chill, she remembered that her cat's ashes were in a tin box in the room directly above her . . . Woooooo!

This story was told to me first hand. Many years ago, my friend's family cat died of old age. She'd been a homely cat in her later years and spent much of her time sleeping in a spare bedroom at the top of the stairs.

Months after her death my friend was watching television when she suddenly strolled in from the garden, glanced at him and wandered up the stairs, disappearing through the open doorway of the spare room.

He sat frozen for a few moments. The sight of her passing through the lounge had been so commonplace until recently, that he hadn't realised at first he was looking at a ghost. He had only an uneasy sense that something was very wrong. This feeling gave way to shock as realisation hit him – the cat that had just climbed the stairs had been dead for some time. He followed slowly up the stairs, his heart beating like a drum, and felt an extreme cold as he approached the spare room.

Bracing himself, he looked into the dimly lit room. It was

completely empty. There was, however, an indentation in the duvet, exactly where she used to sleep.

He told his mother. It turned out she'd seen virtually the same thing a few days earlier, but hadn't wanted to say anything in case it disturbed anyone.

Nothing was seen of her for over a year. The family assumed that she was finally at peace, until they had some friends to stay and put them up in the spare room.

When asked the next morning how they'd slept, thcy said very well but that the cat had disturbed them in the night getting settled beside their feet. They knew nothing of the incidents a year before and assumed they were talking about a current family cat (there wasn't one!).

Everybody was bursting to tell a story by now, and one chap spoke of his Uncle Harry's dog. She died on a winter's day and was buried in the back garden. Late that night, Uncle Harry sat bolt upright in bed. He'd heard barking out in the garden.

Theirs was a very enclosed garden and nobody else nearby had a dog, and in any case, that bark had sounded very familiar. He looked out of the window but could see nothing, only a fresh blanket of snow on the grass. He assumed the sound must have carried from elsewhere and went back to sleep.

He awoke again at around three in the morning. He heard panting and felt hot breath on his face. He sprung out of bed in panic, but there was nothing there. Restless and uneasy, he went downstairs to make a drink. His kitchen light eerily illuminated the white-covered garden outside the window, and he noticed an animal's footprints in the snow. He turned on the outdoor light and went to investigate.

The footprints were definitely those of a dog. They led from the fresh grave, now covered is snow, directly to the back door. There were no footprints leading away – they just stopped right there, as if the dog had walked clean through the locked door.

In the morning his own footprints were still there, from the door to the grave and back again, but there was no sign of the dog's prints. His wife believes that he'd been sleepwalking but he claims he was wide awake and remembers it all as clear as a bell.

I've met the uncle featured in this story many times and whilst knowing him to be honest and true, my only reservation is that the alcohol/supernatural manifestation link would have to be strongly considered here.

Skipping back to my mythical Lakeland cat, we have a bit of a legend here in the Chiltern Hills where we live. A black, panther-like cat is said to stalk these hills and is renowned for its sudden appearances and disappearances.

Way back in April 1983, after sightings near the village of Stokenchurch in Bucks, it was taken so seriously that the local police used helicopters, marksmen and search-parties in an attempt to track it down. The phantom nature of its sudden vanishings has also been the subject of paranormal investigations.

Over the years the sightings have dwindled, but there was almost certainly *something* out there back then. Sheep were savaged and killed (as if sheep didn't already have enough to worry about around here) and large cat-like prints were found. Casts were made of the prints but a species was never established.

Interestingly, I don't know of any sightings since Peanuts moved into its immediate vicinity. I must ask his owners if they ever found a peculiarly large dismembered paw and a long black tail in the office before I knew them. That would explain a lot, especially if the phantom hadn't had time to hide behind a revolving chair.

Cats have long been associated with the supernatural of course, with witchcraft and superstitions and the like. They have managed to give themselves, or we've given them, quite a sinister reputation over the years.

Try as I might I can't look at Brum and think 'sinister'. It just doesn't fit. Would he be more sinister if he came back as a ghost? I wonder . . .

. . . A dark night. We are sitting at home in the lounge. The wind is blowing and our security light goes on outside. It always used to go on when Brum was still around and jumped onto the wall – before falling ten feet over the other side – God rest his soul. We hear a resounding crash. What was that? We go out and take a look. Nothing.

A little later, the security light comes on again, there's another great crash. Nothing's out there. We're perplexed.

The following evening Maya is chattering to herself in the corner. She suddenly swipes at thin air with her new wooden hammer. We hear a thump as if something has fallen heavily to the floor beside her. Very odd. Maya stands and starts viciously kicking at an empty space on the carpet. We hear another sound – like something staggering towards the door. Sammy swipes angrily at nothing in the corridor, must have been a fly or something. We hear the cat-flap bang open and shut. The security light comes on and there's an almighty crash. No, I don't think he'd be very frightening really.

Neither do I think he'd come and haunt us anyway. I think he'd have had enough by then, could do with the rest. I can't see Sammy rising from the grave either. She rarely rises from the bed. When that cat sleeps, she really sleeps. I'm not even sure she isn't dead already.

So, I doubt we'll be bothered particularly by either of them from the other side but I can, however, appreciate that Sammy is perfectly sinister enough in life. She has a staring, scowling look about her that helps me understand why people once feared these creatures, and why Brum still does.

Do cats see ghosts? They look as if they do. In fact Brum's whole style is based on someone who's just seen a ghost. Cats *do* seem to see things we don't though. What about the way cats stare at nothing, suddenly. We all stare at nothing now and then, but why would anybody find nothing so interesting that they should feel the need to stare at it suddenly?

Unless, it's not nothing.

My own opinion is that they don't see ghosts. I don't think they're staring at anything in a startled way, they're listening in a startled way. They're only staring because they're concentrating on a noise they heard and we couldn't.

They may well sense a spirit's presence, but that's a different matter. Animals are often credited with a sixth sense and this may well be true, but Brum hasn't got the hang of the senses he has. I don't think he'd have space for another one.

If you take anything at all from this chapter, it should be this:

If, one dark night as you're walking home alone through the woods, you see the disembodied black shadow of a huge cat in the moonlight, keeping pace with your every step, stalking you . . . you're probably pissed.

The Hall of Fame

'Greatness knows itself.'

Shakespeare

Our washing/utility room is decorated in the style of a very small pub. We have (un)skilfully masked tumble dryers and the like to blend in to the country pub image we're trying to achieve. We've got a Sweaty Betty's Old Ale hand pump (a discontinued black, strong, syrupy beer that should have carried a government health warning. You were once limited to three pints of it at our local, which was a totally pointless rule as anybody who'd downed three pints of the stuff could no more make it to the bar for a fourth than they could get into the ambulance on their own), a pub sign, foreign currency all over the walls (obligatory), beer mats, the works.

It's a tiny pub that looks uncannily like a utility room, but it's pretty cosy and fits nicely with my beer-worshipping ideals.

At one end of this 'pub' we have a rogues' gallery of cats, consisting of small framed photos of various cats who, for one reason or other have earned the right to be there.

Brum is up there of course, caught mid-yawn so he appears to be laughing raucously at the camera. Brum's hard-as-nails live-in-partner-girl-cat Sammy is obviously there too. But others are there for reasons other than the extremely localised fame they've achieved simply through living with us.

Bagpuss, for instance, has his picture on the wall. Bagpuss is Sammy's mentor. Sammy possibly sleeps longer than even Bagpuss, but they definitely have one thing in common. When Sammy wakes up, all her friends wake up. She achieves this similarity by thundering up and down our wooden floored hall in the middle of the night like a herd of charging rhinos. She wakes Maya and Maya lets us know she's awake. We seldom then sit discussing objects that Maya has found and establishing what they might be, however, and if Charlie Mouse were to turn up and start singing songs about it all, then Sammy would tear him to pieces and eat him without hesitation (if she got to him before I did).

A not so well known picture in the Hall of Fame is a magazine cutting of a cat who made his name in the courier industry. Having said that, the Hall of Infamy or the Chamber of Horrors would be a better home for any image of this lad.

His moment came while I was in the business and successfully guiding our own courier company to near disaster. The story was quite a famous one. He was the cat who brought down an entire national courier network.

The network was a hundred-company franchise, overseen by one man in Manchester who acted as the 'hub'. The member companies all pumped their information to a modem he kept in his attic. The information was then made available for all other members of the franchise to take the work relating to their own area. This was before the days of easy internet access and quite a brilliant and innovative system.

The man in Manchester was making a fortune. He didn't even have to do anything, except correct the odd glitch in the system, glitches that were usually minor and very, very rare. He was eventually so sure of the smooth running of his system that he took a two-week holiday abroad, leaving his modem safely running in the attic and his cat being fed by a neighbour. Unfortunately the cat got into the attic which had been left a little too easily accessible, stood on a button and . . . switched off the modem.

One hundred courier companies stared at blank screens.

No one could get hold of the man in Manchester. He believed himself to be contactable on a phone in his holiday home, but unbeknown to him, its ringer was switched off.

The system remained down for twelve days, by which time half of the franchisees had gone bankrupt and the other half had joined other systems.

The man in Manchester was ruined, and so were about fifty courier companies all baying for blood and taking legal action.

What a quality cat that must have been. This happened about

ten years ago and I wonder if he's still around today. One suspects that he would have been lucky to have still been around nine years ago. How could you deal with a cat that had lost you your fortune and put you in court?

'Here Tiddles, biscuits, biscuits, bastard, bastard, BASTARD!'

The Hall of Fame wouldn't be complete without a few family photos. Penny and Batman are commemorated here (Batman could also so easily have been in the Chamber of Horrors, her screeching wax effigy depicted leaping at a helpless drunk in a dimly lit alleyway) as are Brum's parents Paris and Camber – if you cross your eyes when you look at them and merge the two cats into one, you actually get a very good likeness of the lad himself. Another little insight into the strangeness of my ways there, hanging around in pretend pubs pulling cross-eyed faces at pictures of deceased cats.

An old cat of Lorraine's, Cat-Cat, has a slot waiting for her, when Lorraine can find a picture. I'm told in warmth of nature, she was a lot like Brum, but thankfully for her, the similarity ended there. Brum's brother Lester will also have a place, and my sister is getting us a photo of him. I would hope Lester himself doesn't turn up with it. One weird cat is enough for any household, without his invisible brother moving in.

I'd also have put up a picture of my favourite fictional cat of all time, from the Tom Holt comic fantasy novel *Flying Dutch*, but this would mean cutting up the book cover, so I won't. This cat was not only harder than Peanuts, Sammy and a couple of tigers rolled into one, he was hundreds of years old, smelt to high heaven and was immortal, doomed to sail the seas for eternity with the rest of the crew of the Flying Dutchman. He was probably the vilest cat in any book I've ever read, but also the funniest. Last but not least of those deserving a place, are a couple of extraordinary world-record-breaking felines.

Brum may have an incredible tenacity for hanging on to his precarious existence, but I somehow doubt he'll live to break the world age record currently held by a tabby named Ma, who lived to the age of 35, or if you use the old seven years cat/human year conversion – 245! Even then, after 245 years, she wasn't intending to go anywhere. She was finally put to sleep.

It must've been the only way of stopping her.

Finally, one space will forever stay empty in honour of a cat imaginatively named 'Pussycat' who earned his own place in the *Guinness Book of Records* when, in 1965, surpassing all others in the great fall stakes, he 'slipped and fell 120 feet from the balcony of an eleventh floor flat, and survived'.

'Slipped and fell 120 feet.' Style personified. There's one even Brum could have learnt a thing or two from.

Pet Passports

'To travel hopefully is better than to arrive.'

Sir James Jeans

Brum hasn't applied for one of those Pet Passports as yet. Whether that's because he's just never fancied going abroad for his holidays, or because he's a cat and therefore has no awareness of passports, holidays, abroad or even of applications, I don't know.

He's only ever had UK holidays and all were enforced. One was in a cattery for a long weekend. It was a luxury cattery, with spacious accommodation, en-suite litter room, three-course meals and live cabaret.

The cabaret consisted of a series of hamster runs set up in front of the cats' pens so that they had something to look at. However pleasant you try to make it all, it was still three days in a wire cage being tortured by small furry creatures agonisingly out of reach.

When we arrived to collect him, he saw us and began screaming at us, possibly abusively, as we entered the garden. He was absolutely distraught. The warden told us he had been thoroughly miserable the whole time. We felt as guilty as hell. He complained all the way home and, I think as an act of protest, was sick on the bed the moment we got in.

The cattery was good, and most of the cats looked thoroughly content, but it just wasn't for him. It was decided to never put him through anything like that again, and he has stayed at my parents' for his (our) holidays ever since.

The thought of him taking an imaginary package tour is quite amusing, however. I wonder which destinations would be right for him.

One of my favourites has always been Greece, but I'm not sure he'd like it there one bit. For a start the accommodation. There isn't any. While some people own cats in Greece, the majority of them live rough and scavenge for their food around bins and restaurants (the cats, not the Greeks).

They are generally a skinny and mangy looking lot, and again it's the cats I'm referring to. I think he'd either starve to death or be murdered by the mean looking locals. Local *cats* of course – bloody hell, I just can't seem to talk about, or to, Greeks for five seconds without accidentally insulting them or their families. What is it with me? I've never seemed to get on too well with them as it is, without suggesting, in print, that they're a nation of dustbin raiding cat murderers.

I don't know why I don't get on with them, they just don't seem to like me. Something in my manner upsets Greeks. Nowhere else in Europe do I have this problem, just in Greece. If I'd been a diplomat during the Classical Era and sent to negotiate peace and trade with Athens, I'd have immediately outraged my welcoming hosts and instigated a trade embargo followed by all-out war. So, to the people of Greece: sorry, okay, for whatever it is I do. But I'm sure you will agree that many of you do have dodgy moustaches, and that's not nice is it? And Retsina should only be used to store gherkins in. That's all.

Greece is off the list then. No accommodation, little chance of food (especially now).

How about America? Nice and civilised. They love cats out there. I even know people in Texas who would have him over to stay for a few weeks (a sign of madness). But would Brum survive a few weeks in Texas?

The people would be good to him. He'd have plenty of food. I know from bitter-sweet experience that a Texas 'starter' is enough to feed an average family of four for a week.

It's the wildlife in Texas that would finish him. Everything in Texas wants to 'get' you. The reptiles, insects, even the plants. They have a particularly nasty stinging insect called the fire ant, which originally came from Mexico. It was once demonstrated to me just how fast these things are. My friend poked a long stick into a fire ant mound and let go almost immediately.

The ants were at the top of the stick, in huge numbers, before it hit the ground.

They are excessively aggressive and were attempting to attack. They clamp onto their victim with their jaws and then sting them repeatedly, and the sting is nasty. I was stung by one once and the effect was very much like having a naked flame held millimetres below your skin for far too long. Having a number of fire ants sting you at once almost certainly explains the origins of Hillbilly dancing.

Their mounds are now on most Texan lawns, and they are extremely dangerous to cats and dogs. From the example of the stick demonstration, I can clearly imagine how horrific it would be for a pet to be a little too curious around a mound, and I just know Brum would be stretching out on one within seconds. But, if the old saying 'no sense, no feeling' were true, he'd probably stay on it all day. I can easily visualise him sitting there, hind leg continually scratching at his ears, head in the air, wondering why he's feeling a little itchy.

As if these terrible ants weren't danger enough for Brum, he can choose from rattlesnakes (the rattle would be bound to interest him), water moccasins (snakes that don't even try to warn you off, just want to fight you to the death for a laugh), coyotes, black widow spiders, all manner of malicious plants, even alligators.

For a lad who's grown up with nothing much more dangerous than grass snakes, mice and sparrows, and still come off worse, I wouldn't bank on him ever needing to present his Pet Passport back in the UK. I think they could pretty much write him off the moment he landed at Dallas International.

So, cross out Greece and America.

How about Egypt? A popular destination for cats for over 4,000 years. The cradle of cat civilisation. What a great cultural holiday for a cat. He could gaze at cat statues (some still survive) and visit the site of the temple of the cat god Bastet.

But is Egypt as hospitable a place for a cat as it was in 2500 BC? Now, in keeping with the people of Slough, Egyptians don't worship cats any more. The majority of the population are apparently unaware they're supposed to. But they *are* still very polite to cats and generally provide food to cats that ask.

Urban cats are very popular. The fact that the people are so fond of cats and seem to still feel protective towards them has led to Egyptian cities having an enormous, out-of-control cat population. I once read an article saying that cats roam about in most public buildings and are all over the stage in concert halls and theatres, often proving more interesting than the action going on around them. They are even rumoured to have infested the Halls of Power in Egypt and sit in on most Government meetings (possibly they *are* still in charge?). I've since seen this report denied by an Egyptian Government official, who did however admit, after appearing to consult with a small, pointy eared, furry colleague, that there is indeed a bit of a problem with the huge quantities of homeless cats in Egypt.

An Egyptian city for your next holiday Brum? No, too overcrowded.

Many parts of the Egyptian countryside have an entirely different attitude to cats, however. Whereas Egyptian townies will happily stroke and pet cats, country folk tend to still treat them with a degree of reverence. Many villagers believe it is wrong to touch a cat. I would say it's okay myself. Wrong to touch cobras. Okay to touch cats. But there is still an uneasy superstition surrounding them that has kept cats sacred if not worshipped.

Brum wouldn't care for their attitude at all. He'd take it as a personal affront. Good place for Sammy to reaffirm her opinion of herself as a demi-god though.

Greece, America and Egypt not suitable. Where next?

How about Australia? Cats officially arrived in Australia with the First Fleet in 1788, although it's now believed that castaway cats from Dutch shipwrecks probably got there first – with maybe a particularly stinky, tough and immortal one among their numbers? It's possible that some may have arrived even earlier with Indonesian fishermen.

Australia wanted more cats a little while back. In the late

nineteenth century they imported as many as they could and let them loose in the bush and outback. Why? To try to kill off the rabbits they'd already imported and let loose in the bush and outback, where they'd bred to epidemic proportions and started eating the entire country. Attack of the continent-eating bunnies.

The cats (and imported foxes) killed plenty of them, but not enough. Various viruses have also been used and the latest Calici virus is doing the job. Unfortunately as Calici dramatically reduces the rabbit population, it also reduces the amount of food available for Australia's five million feral cats. These cats will eventually have to start eating other Australian species to make up the shortfall. Taking the rabbit population down was intended to have a knock-on control effect on cat and fox populations, which it probably will have, but the cats and foxes will go down fighting and take many others with them.

A bit of a feline battleground. You don't want to go on holiday to the only cat warzone on the planet, do you? Okay, that's exactly where you'd expect to find our Brum, but I can't see him liking the outback much in any case. He does actually have the natural equipment to survive there should he wish to. Cats take enough moisture from their prey to enable them to go without drinking water, so they *can* survive those arid and inhospitable conditions.

But why the hell would he want to? He'd never catch anything. If he'd been one of the first new cats out there, hunting in a landscape absolutely wall to wall with rabbits, he'd be jumping around arch-backed all over the place without ever catching a damn thing.

And then he'd get stomped by a kangaroo in a cork hat.

Despite cats threatening to destroy their ecology, Australians in towns and cities tend to love them to bits. One in three homes have cats. So Sydney or Melbourne would be fine, but the local deadly wildlife count is Texas times ten.

Everything on and around the Australian Continent seems geared to killing everything else. Australia is home to the world's top ten deadliest snakes, the world's deadliest spiders, instant-death jellyfish, toxic octopuses, tons of lethal insects, killer fish, poisonous plants, venomous crustaceans, man-eating crocodiles, vicious birds, Australian Rules Football and one of the most inhospitably sun-baked climates on the planet. Take an environment where absolutely everything is trying to kill you, and place into it a cat determined to kill himself (albeit unintentionally) and you have a recipe for instant destruction.

Forget Australia.

Oh, and if anybody from any Australian Environment committees is reading, here are some unnecessary tips:

1. Don't release rabbits into your countryside.
2. Don't try and correct your first mistake by releasing other mistakes into your countryside.
3. Don't hide behind true excuses like 'some pillock of an English landowner started it all, not us'.
4. Don't tell me my advice is over a hundred years too late.
5. And if you ever have rabbit problems again, you only need ask. We'll send you Peanuts. Not only would he solve your problem in weeks, he doesn't tend to breed too much any more and you'll have a 'lucky rabbit foot' trade that's second to none. When you've finished with his services, just litter the Outback with office swivel chairs and he'll trouble you no more.

Really, these colonials. Leave 'em to their own devices and look what happens . . .

Right, so the Australians and Greeks don't like me or my stinking opinions (or my cat and his stinking opinions), America's too dangerous and the Egyptians have got enough cat problems without my inflicting Brum on them. Okay, grab another brochure, plenty more world yet.

Mexico? No. Latin American fire-ant dancing is even more embarrassing than its Hillbilly cousin.

Russia? Russia, now there's a possibility.

In Russia, to have a cat in the house is seen as a sign of good luck (they haven't met Brum, have they?). Cats are very popular pets, and in Moscow there is a Cat Museum, showing permanent displays of cat art, the cats being in the pictures rather than having painted them.

What's more, the Russians seem to be genuine cat lovers.

They have an abundance of cat fancier clubs, many of whom have recently been celebrating the recognition of the 'Siberian' as a 'Standard Breed' by Federation International Felines (FIFE), which I've never heard of but presume they oversee worldwide feline football events. The tabbies versus the white cats, that sort of thing.

The Siberian is a fluffy type of tabby that looks incredibly, amazingly like Brum. I saw it described as 'sweet natured'. Could they mean daft and dopey, possibly? I decided to find out more about this breed. If they do mean daft and dopey, could this be what Brum is, and not a prehistoric missing link after all?

Are there thousands like him in Russian Asia, blundering across the Tundra, walking into wind blasted trees and falling down Mammoth excavation pits?

The first details I found were encouraging:

1. Thick coat, full ruff:	Correct.
2. Doglike:	Author didn't elaborate on what he meant by 'doglike' but if he meant doglike as lacking the balance and agility of a cat, then correct.
3. Oily coat:	I'm not sure about this one. He isn't exactly oily but I wouldn't say he feels beautiful and clean either.
4. Not fond of other cats' company:	That's right.
5. Loyal and affectionate:	Yes, he is!

I looked up another site and the results weren't so good, they did however explain some rather vague descriptions in the first.

1. Thick coat, full ruff:	Yes, yes, we know.
2. Large, strong:	NO WAY!
3. Oily, water-resistant coat:	WATER-RESISTANT!! No.
4. Kitten is size of a normal cat:	What? The pictures I saw must have been of kittens then. What size do they grow to for goodness sake, are we talking about Siberian Tabbies or Siberian Tigers here?
5. Fearless:	No. I'm getting depressed now.
6. Guards house like an Alsatian dog:	Losing interest.
7. Used to live in the high rafters of monasteries, skipping expertly between the thin beams, always on the lookout for intruders:	!

Okay, that's enough. Until I hear anything to the contrary, he's a miacis. I tried.

The info I obtained may have been useful in some respects however. If Brum is going to Russia, he's going to be dwarfed by the locals. From the description of the Siberian it sounds like he'd be best advised not to get into any fights unless he's heavily armed.

Another angle he should consider here is espionage. I know the Cold War is officially over, but there still lingers that slight air of suspicion.

He does, however much he differs in size, look incredibly like a Siberian. When the Russians see him they're immediately going to suspect him of being a Western spy in a silly Siberian disguise.

Sean Connery disguised as Japanese in *Diamonds are Forever* springs to mind. He was about two foot taller and wider than everybody he was with. He looked ridiculous. Brum would look just as odd hanging out with a bunch of Siberians. He'll be like a perfectly proportioned miniature. He'd never pull it off.

Amazingly Sean Connery did fool the bad guys for a while in his disguise, but he certainly didn't fool anybody else.

Right, Russia's off the list, he'd be arrested or torn to pieces by huge effigies of himself. There must be somewhere he could go.

There is . . . my mum's. It's about the only safe option. They're aware of what he's capable of, so have extensive medical supplies available for when he comes to stay. And they don't have alligators lurking in their fish pond.

Even if we had found a suitable destination for him, he'd have never got travel insurance. They'd have asked questions such as: Will you be participating in any dangerous activities . . .

Yes. Everything he does is a dangerous activity. Walking is a dangerous activity. Massively dangerous. Eating and sleeping are an absolute minefield.

I can't help feeling as if we're giving up too easily here. Copping out. Maybe we're not trying hard enough. If we paid more for insurance and racked our brains for a place he wouldn't definitely get himself killed in . . .

What time shall I drop you off at my mum's, Brum?

The Anti-Sunday Boy

'The height of cleverness,
is to be able to conceal it.'

Duc de le Rochefoucauld

One major thing with many of Brum's accidents is that they don't always have the effect that he so richly deserves them to have, i.e. he gets hurt, others don't.

With one simple action, Brum is capable of setting into motion a chain of events that lead to calamity. The first that springs to mind happened just the other day . . .

It was a relaxing Sunday morning. Lorraine was reading the newspaper and I was chatting to my Mum on the phone while having a coffee. Sammy was out cold beside the fire and baby Maya taking a nap in her room. It seemed a scene of domestic bliss, but Brum was looking twitchy. Sitting alone in an armchair and nervously watching everybody in the room, he had that look about him. It's a look that most cat owners may be familiar with, a sort of 'Oh my God, I've just realised I'm sitting on a landmine' type look.

And in much the same way as you would if you had just sat on a landmine, Brum suddenly and without warning shot high into the air, landed on my lap and sprung on over my shoulder at desperate speed.

This would have been fine except that he neglected to avoid the telephone handset cable, thus taking the receiver and my right hand with him.

That my mouth was at that point connected to a full cup of hot coffee made things much much worse.

One moment I was sitting, chatting on the phone and calmly sipping coffee, the next my hand shot up and backwards over my head, the other hand automatically trying to go with it and pouring a full cup of coffee straight into my face.

In considerable pain and swearing loudly, I hopped up and

down. My Mum put the phone down, disgusted by my language, a startled Sammy left the room without touching the floor, Lorraine's newspaper was smothered in coffee and a little voice boomed WAAAAAAAAHHH over the monitor.

Laughing boy, meanwhile, was calmly washing his arse in the kitchen.

So you see what I mean. That's what he's capable of. Another incident involving liquid in much larger quantities occurred during the summer.

This incident also happened on a Sunday. I don't know if Brum hates Sunday morning rituals, such as the following, and makes it his sworn duty to disrupt them, or it's just that I happen to see more of him on Sundays and he's always like this.

I was out in the drive washing the car with sponge, bowl and hosepipe whilst chatting with my neighbour who was doing much the same sort of thing – washing his car-cum-cat-surfboard.

Brum was out there with me and enjoying a little game of snakes and tabbies. Snakes and tabbies is a simple game. It occurs because I have to leave my hosepipe nozzle half on. If I don't, pressure builds and rips the other end of the hose from the tap. This practice causes the hosepipe to slither around like a snake as the water slowly escapes, thus causing the tabby to chase it.

All was well until about the third time I lifted the hosepipe and turned the nozzle to jetblast. It appears that Brum hadn't quite finished with it and launched himself at a piece of hosepipe about six inches off the ground and just behind me, gripping it and hauling it to the ground.

The effect on my nozzle was quite dramatic.

The hose being suddenly ripped from my hands made me grab at it and pull it up and forwards, sending a sudden stream of water towards my totally unaware neighbour, whom it thankfully missed, hitting an old lady square in the back as she walked past his drive.

I meanwhile stepped forward into my bowl of water, tipping it up and drenching my trouser legs.

The sudden explosions of water sent Brum running for cover

whilst I headed inside for a change of clothing. Behind me I could hear the old lady remonstrating with my neighbour about soaking her coat, something which he seemed to be confessing to. I think this was probably because he was holding a hosepipe and felt an innocent plea would have looked ridiculous.

Nobody saw the dodgy-looking bloke sneaking away in his sodden trousers, or the tabby beneath the bush, grinning happily, his secret objective achieved – another peaceful weekend tradition had been sabotaged by the Anti-Sunday Boy.

A Chat With a Cat

(A Fantasy Interview)

'Ain't it grand to be blooming well dead.'

Leslie Sarony

The setting: a weird, 'afterlife'-style, foggy, surreal room. Brum's latest disaster has resulted in the untimely demise of both cat and owner in annoyingly ridiculous circumstances.

CP: Good evening, Brum.

B: Good evening, Chris.

CP: Now that you've finally managed to kill us both, and we find ourselves strangely able to communicate with one another on more than a 'feed me/get down' level, I thought it might be a good idea to look back over your life, your highs and lows, your viewpoints and perspectives, how a cat sees our world . . .

B: Your world?

CP: Sorry?

B: You said your world, I presume you mean that the world belongs to human beings. That's a little species elitist, isn't it?

CP: Okay, sorry, point taken. Anyway, my idea was that we conduct a formal interview. I've a set of questions already written out.

B: Good evening!

CP: Er right, the questions I've set out are aimed at establishing an in-depth picture of how a cat thinks, of your dreams, aspirations and ambitions. Some of the questions may be fairly provocative but . . .

B: I'm not answering anything about the white cat.

CP: Okay.

B: Proceed.

CP: What would you say was the best pair of shoes you ever owned?

B: What?

CP: Your best ever pair of shoes?

B: Where did you get your questions from?

CP: Okay, what's your favourite colour then?

B: Oh, I don't know . . . white.

CP: White isn't a colour.

B: Of course it is.

CP: It's not actually.

B: Look is this question relevant, I mean, I'm a cat. I don't even see in colour.

CP: Oh yeah, that's right isn't it. What do you think would be your favourite colour if you could see in colour.

B: Can we just move on please.

CP: Who is your all-time favourite pop star?

B: Have you got the right set of questions?

CP: Yes.

B: Sir Cliff Richard or Eminem. Both really. I'd like to have seen them do a duet.

CP: What would you say was the greatest day of your life?

B: The day you took me away from Slough.

CP: That's very nice of you, thank you.

B: It wasn't a compliment. If you'd been Genghis Khan and you'd taken me away to cook me alive and eat me it would still have been the greatest day of my life.

CP: What was the worst day of your life?

B: Today's been pretty bad.

CP: Don't start me on today again, what the bloody hell were you thinking of anyway. Sometimes you're a total . . .

B: Okay, okay, calm down. Worst day, worst day. Hmmm, tricky one. Ah, I know. The day I was left dangling over the side of the wall for two whole hours, attached to that lead weight, and the RSPCA came and arrested you and you beat up that monkey.

CP: None of those things happened Brum.

B: Didn't they?

CP: No. That was a fantasy scenario earlier in the book. You couldn't possibly even have known about that scenario.

B: No, no, you're right. Okay, I think it would have been the day that I was stung by a wasp and fell out of the window at the flat.

CP: Ah, so you *were* stung by a wasp! I wondered about that.

B: Hmmm, anyway, that would have been about the worst.

CP: Really, I can think of a lot worse things that happened to you than that, what about the day you . . .

B: Can we move on?

CP: What about the day your head caught fire? That must have been pretty horrendous?

B: No, it was fine, I enjoyed it, can we move on please?

CP: Or the day you got hit by the bicycle and the paperboy went face first into next door's flowerbed.

B: That wasn't my fault, he was riding on the pavement.

CP: He said it was your fault. The postman said you ran straight out in front of him. Poor kid grazed his knee quite badly.

B: He was riding on the pavement. There are bye-laws, you know, bye-laws. If he wants to ride on the pavement, *he* should have been looking out for *me*. I could have been an old lady or something. If I'd been an old lady, everyone would have said 'Ooo, it's terrible, he shouldn't have been riding on that pavement, it's so dangerous.' But instead it's, 'It's that stupid cat's fault again,' regardless of the fact that I had right of way. *It was my right of way!*

CP: An old lady wouldn't have jumped out of the bushes at ninety miles an hour straight in front of his wheels would she?!

B: Move on please.

CP: Is white your favourite colour because Sammy's white?

B: One, white is not a colour, and two, you weren't going to ask me anything about the white cat.

CP: You can call her Sammy. Her name's Sammy, not 'the white cat'.

B: I know her as the white cat.

CP: Wouldn't you have said that the day you got beaten by a sparrow was the worst day?

B: No.

CP: It must have been the most humiliating.

B: No. I felt much more humiliated having to watch you sitting in that puddle and making a fool of yourself in front of the farmer and his bodyguard.

CP: Oh, very cutting Brum, very cutting. Anyway, that was his son, not his bodyguard.

B: Ohhhhh, well, that's all right then. Not humiliating at all in that case!

CP: You put me in that bloody puddle anyway.

B: *Well, you didn't tell me there was going to be a snorting great monster in the shed, did you.* If you'd shared that little piece of *vital* information with me, then none of it would have happened.

CP: Right, let's calm this down a little. Next question.

B: Hallelujah!

CP: What's your favourite food?

B: Oh mercy. Tuna.

CP: Did you resent being neutered?

B: I beg your pardon?

CP: Did you resent being neutered?

B: What does neutered mean?

CP: You know . . . ?

B: No, I don't.

CP: Okay, next question. What is your all-time favourite film?

B: Er, I didn't really watch television. What does neutered mean?

CP: You watched football.

B: Only Norwich City, and they were rubbish most of the time. What does neutered mean? Tell me?

CP: Oh God, um, it's er, difficult. Didn't you think, one day, that things were suddenly a bit different, um y'know, down there?

B: Down where? Back on earth? What things?

CP: No. Down . . . there?

B: What are you pointing at?

CP: Let's move on. We'll talk about this later, okay. Now, what made you babysit for Maya, I mean, we were very grateful and everything, but what caused you to be so . . . useful?

B: Do you mean the small, large-headed one?

CP: Yes.

B: Well, she used to call for me and I used to go to her, that's all.

CP: Ah, so you thought she was calling to you?

B: She was calling to me.

CP: No, no, she was just crying. You just thought she was calling to you.

B: Fine, have it your way. But when someone shouts out 'Brum, can you come here a moment' clear as a bell, I would say they were calling to me, but whatever you like, you're the big intelligent human who owns the world, after all . . .

CP: Wait a minute, wait a minute. Are you saying that you could understand what Maya was saying to you?

B: Yes, most of what she said.

CP: Which bits didn't you understand?

B: The bits in your language. But she didn't know your language very well anyway. I told her that there was nothing you'd say that'd be worth hearing anyway . . .

CP: *This is fantastic.* Maya could speak your language. All these years everybody thought that babies were just making random sounds and they were speaking . . . Cat. You know what this means don't you Brummy Boy?

B: No. Enlighten me Chrissy Lad.

CP: We, my furry friend, are going to be rich and famous. We need to make sure we get this patented. This is the scientific breakthrough of the century. We could make millions out of this!

B: Too late. We're dead.

CP: Sod it!

B: Life's a bitch, and then you die.

CP: No, wait, wait. You're forgetting something. We're – not – really – dead. I made it all up for this interview, remember?

B: Yes. And – you – made – this – interview – up – too. Remember?

CP: That doesn't matter. No hang on, it does matter. *Dammit*. I made up the bit about babies speaking Cat too, didn't I?

B: Yep.

CP: I don't believe it, I could almost taste the money then Brum.

B: Well, at least we've still got our health, that's the main thing, aye.

CP: Hmmm, yes, I suppose it is.

B: None too intelligent just then though, were you kidda?

CP: Pressing onwards. What would you say was the worst thing about being a cat?

B: The hours.

CP: No, seriously?

B: The worst thing for me was having to socialise with other cats. I just never felt like I was a cat.

CP: Hmmm, yes, more miacis than cat really.

B: What does that mean?

CP: No nothing, just thinking aloud, carry on.

B: That's it really. I didn't like cats much. Had no real sense of felinity. You know that dog in the James Herbert book, *Fluke*?

CP: Yes.

B: He didn't think he was a cat.

CP: He wasn't.

B: No. That's right . . .

Silence

CP: What was the best thing about being a cat?

B: The hours.

CP: Sigh.

B: It really was the hours this time. Definitely the hours.

CP: Okay. If you could bottle a smell what would it be?

B: You wouldn't like the answer to that one. Our cultural differences would render the answer unpalatable to you.

CP: I had no idea that you supported Norwich City.

B: Well, I didn't support them exactly, just liked to see the games. Cheer them on a bit, you know.

CP: Why Norwich City?

B: Nickname appealed first off I suppose, the Canaries, but after that I don't know really . . .

CP: Delia Smith supports Norwich you know?

Silence

CP: I supported Watford.

Silence

CP: Having this lively chat about football with you reminds me of another good candidate for your worst day ever. How about the day you went out with those knickers wrapped around you? You must have felt a right pillock that day. Lazing on top of the car in front of all those Wycombe supporters on their way down to the ground, with a pair of lacey knickers slung round your neck. We only realised what was going on when one lot started singing 'Are you Beckham in disguise?'

B: The large-headed one put them on me.

CP: We think, we don't know.

B: For the purposes of this interview and my vanity, we know.

CP: And the really good bit was when we opened the door and you ran up the steps with your knickers flying in the air and they all wolf whistled you and shouted things like 'Get 'em off darling!' . . . Boy, must you have felt humiliated that day.

B: You are really beginning to annoy me Pascoe.

CP: You know, now I think about it, the amount of things you've done like that, that haven't been included in the book, is pretty staggering. I hadn't mentioned the paperboy crash, or the knicker incident until now. Or the thing with the lawn mower. Or the thing with the inflatable banana when you broke the lamp and lost part of your left ear, or . . .

B: Right, that's it, I'm out of here.

CP: What are your views on religion?

B: What?

CP: Your views on religion, what are they? I'd be very interested to know. Do you have a religion? What do cats believe? Is there a cat God? Is he the same God as ours? Do cats believe in an afterlife? Heaven and hell? Are certain things sacred to you?

B: Are you really wanting to know or is this just the lead up to another piss take about things long past? Or some stupid question like 'What's your all-time favourite item of clothing?'

CP: I really want to know.

B: Well, fundamentally we believe in . . .

CP: *Nah!* Had you going, don't really want to know. What's your all-time favourite item of clothing?

B: I'm answering the first one now. Fundamentally we believe in the same God as you. We believe in one God, one Eternal Spirit who . . .

CP: And is he furry?

B: Could you give me your hand a moment?

CP: Sure, why? Aaaahh! That flipping hurt. That's bleeding now.

B: . . . watches over us. We believe that upon death we go to a much better place . . .

CP: What, here?

B: No, when we're really dead, we go to a place much like your Heaven, only chock full of small defenceless animals and flightless birds.

CP: Not much of a Heaven for the small defenceless animals and flightless birds is it?

B: It's their hell.

CP: Oh, I see. And is there a cat hell? Is that full of horrible great monster birds with razor talons and vicious beaks?

B: How peculiar that you should think a cat hell would be peopled by your ex-girlfriends. No. We don't need a hell. Cats believe that a cat is perfection personified, faultless and blameless in every perceivable way.

CP: And you *really* believe that, do you?

B: The white cat does.

CP: What is your all-time favourite item of clothing?

B: I'm not doing that one.

CP: Did you have any heroes when you were younger?

B: You got these questions from some teenage girls' magazine didn't you? You read teenage girls' magazines, do you Chris?

CP: When did you first start using make-up?

B: When was my first kiss?

CP: When was your first kiss?

B: Hang on a minute.

CP: What?

B: Does neutered mean clumsy? Were you asking if I resented being clumsy? Only, I don't think I was clumsy. I think people around me were clumsy. Especially you and the small large-headed one.

CP: Er, yes, well neutered does indeed mean clumsy, and you're probably right in what you say.

B: I know I'm right. I think that the paperboy was neutered when he fell off his bike. I think that your friend at the farm was neutered that day I jumped on his lap, and I think that you were very definitely neutered the day you fell into the Christmas tree . . . why are you wincing like that?

CP: Look Brum, I'll level with you here. It was only you who was neutered, and possibly the guy at the farm. What it basically means is (*whispers in ear*).

B: !

CP: You understand, do you?

B: !

CP: Brum?

B: Oh my God, oh my God, oh my God. *I was neutered?*

CP: Yes, I thought you knew, I . . .

B: *You bastard! You complete bastard!*

CP: Calm down!

B: *No! Interview closed.* And all that time I thought that I'd just gone off the boil. That would have been about the time I developed that love of wild flowers and started purring a lot. It all makes sense now.

CP: Look, just calm down will you . . .

B: *Shut it you, outside right now!*

CP: Where's the door?

B: No idea, it's all foggy in here.

This interview was conducted under strict netherworld conditions. A copy of the full, uncensored sound recording is available from all good record shops at a price of £1.50. But only in the afterlife. So if you're dying to hear it, that would be about right.